Governors State University
Library Hours:
Monday thru Thursday 8:00 to 10:30
Friday 8:00 to 5:00
Saturday 8:30 to 5:00
Sunday 1:00 to 5:00 (Fall
and Winter Trimester Only)

Collaborative Action Research

Collaborative Action Research

Developing Professional Learning Communities

Edited by

STEPHEN P. GORDON

Foreword by
Emily F. Calhoun

Teachers College, Columbia University
New York and London

Published by Teachers College Press, 1234 Amsterdam Avenue, New York, NY 10027

Library of Congress Cataloging-in-Publication Data

Collaborative action research : developing professional learning communities / edited by Stephen P. Gordon.
   p. cm.
  Includes bibliographical references and index.
  ISBN 978-0-8077-4898-5 (pbk. : alk. paper)
  ISBN 978-0-8077-4899-2 (hardcover : alk. paper)
    1. Action research in education. 2. Group work in education. I. Gordon, Stephen P., 1948–

  LB1028.24.C655   2008
  370.72—dc22   2008024044

ISBN 978-0-8077-4898-5 (paper)
ISBN 978-0-8077-4899-2 (hardcover)

15   14   13   12   11   10   09   08   8 7 6 5 4 3 2 1

Contents

PART II: The School's Role

Foreword

THE IDEA OF WORKING TOGETHER for the common good of all has been around for a long time. Whether as family members, employees, or citizens, it's a concept that most of us understand. Its application in education has been elegantly described by Schaefer in *The School as a Center of Inquiry* (1967) and by Glickman in *Renewing America's Schools: A Guide for School-Based Action* (1993). Yet few educators and students are in schools where this idea is a cultural attribute of the environment.

Many of us who work in schools, school districts, universities, and public service to children struggle continuously to integrate our work so that we all are learning and supporting students academically and morally through the content and design of instruction and the kind of workplace we create for ourselves. We have good ideas about how to work together, we have good intentions, and we have knowledgeable persons in all organizations involved. So, what's the problem? Why aren't we creating more workplace environments that have as attributes the Principles of the National Center for School Improvement's (NCSI) School Improvement Network (see Figure I.2): an inquiry orientation that continuously questions current practices and seeks new ideas as part of a healthy system of growth and renewal; rigorous and public collective work in developing learning capacity and strengthening curriculum, instruction, and the use of data and information; and a social system designed to support continuous learning and interactions among school-based and university-based educators, students, parents, community members and services, and regional/state agency staff? Why aren't we engaging in more collaborative and schoolwide action research?

My thesis regarding the rarity of collaborative study and action within schools and across organizations is twofold: (a) far too few of us know how to actualize the idea and bring about healthier and more effective ways of working together, and (b) the normative expectations of how schooling works that are held by both educators and other citizens in our society depress collective work. These two major factors function as inhibitors of collective inquiry and action within and across educational organizations. They lead educators and responsible parties to avoid experimentation with the social order, thus keeping many schools locked into their current organizational structure. Early in our country's history, we had one-room schoolhouses; today, we have many large educational institutions—from elementary schools to universities—that function in many ways like a series of one-room schoolhouses under one roof. With all the available technology for supporting communication and collaborative problem-solving, current school design at all levels still promotes individual work to the detriment of collective work.

Much of this book addresses these two factors, especially the first one. The authors describe the integrative power of working together. They publicly announce the principles and goals they value and that guide their workplace interactions. The title of the book, *Collaborative Action Research: Developing Professional Learning Communities*, itself foreshadows those values with words that denote collective inquiry and action, unity of purpose, and expectations of learning and growth for participating individuals and their organizations. These authors share their experiences with collaborative action research, one way of working together to create sustainable learning organizations.

In the Introduction, Gordon invites us to inquire into the power of schoolwide collaborative action research as a school improvement process. As he describes the effects of action research and how he and his colleagues in Texas State University's School Improvement Network work with school faculties, it is easy to see how in-depth inquiry from multiple perspectives provides information for reflection that leads to changes in practice, how learning and solving problems together generate increased respect for self and others, and how the action research cycle of study/reflect/act keeps the learning process dynamic.

In Part I, four authors take us into their experiences as critical friends or supporters of collaborative action research. As a believer in reading (and writing) to learn from and with others, I am often amazed by the distance between desirable practices and current common practices. Such was the case here. As I read each chapter and thought about the different perspectives presented, I wished that every university responsible for graduating teachers and administrators had a program that developed the social skills, problem-solving capacities, ability to reflect on one's own actions and those of others, and leadership skills evident and evolving that are illustrated in these examples of university colleagues and graduate students working with school-based colleagues.

In education today, there is much rhetoric about building leadership and capacity for improvement. Here, instead of rhetoric, we are allowed to stand beside our colleagues and watch how they used schoolwide collaborative action research to build internal capacity through developing informed, distributed leadership. We see how they worked to initiate effective leadership teams and faculty meetings where educators took time to study data, question actions and suggestions, listen to one another, discuss differences, and interact in different ways. They worked to support meetings where participants learn and engage, and challenge themselves and others as they accomplish their tasks—not just meetings where the tasks get done but people leave no different from when they entered the room. Was every move or act successful? Not by any measure. But, of course, that would be the case in real university/school partnerships. As Smyth advocates, would that we had more universities seeking such alliances!

In Part II, eight authors help us take a closer look at what happens as school faculties encounter schoolwide action research. Tradition, culture, readiness for social innovation, leadership, and available support affect its initiation, its implementation, and its durability as a vehicle for individual and organizational development. I especially enjoyed the combination of research reviews and personal experiences that allowed me to see the perspective of the authors as they worked with more and less effective implementers of action research. Their written reflections, shared formally with us here, provide information that can help faculties, leadership teams, administrators, and critical friends/technical assistance providers be more prepared and skillful in using collective inquiry. As we read, we have an opportunity to, as McGhee and Boone advise, use "past and present practice [to] positively inform our work for the future."

Those of us who believe in action research as a form of continuous learning for individuals and renewal for organizations are always on the lookout for resources that can enlighten our efforts. We know the difficulties of supporting school improvement processes that are intellectually effective and morally humane and generative; we are aware that not all believe in, as one author described it, "action-in-common." When we find something that helps us better understand our work, helps us recognize ourselves as part of a larger professional community with common values, and provides tools and hope for self-renewing schools, we feel that we have found treasure. As you read the following chapters, it will be easy to visualize schools filled with intellectual discourse and collective action that unite and move the community forward while avoiding stifling conformity. From the experiences these authors shared, I learned something about how to support the work I value, and I believe you will also.

—Emily F. Calhoun
Director, The Phoenix Alliance

Preface

REFLECTION IS A CRITICAL ASPECT of education on many different levels. Good teachers encourage students to reflect on their lives, their actions, and their learning. Good educational leaders encourage teachers to reflect on their educational beliefs, their teaching, and their professional growth. And those of us who work with educational leaders encourage them to reflect on their leadership platforms, their leadership behaviors, and their goals for the future. We also encourage all members of the school communities we work with to collectively reflect on their school's current level of performance, its vision for the future, and its progress in moving toward that vision.

The authors in this book—university professors, consultants, and K–12 practitioners—were all in some way associated with a school improvement network focused on facilitating schoolwide collaborative action research. Throughout the action research process at these schools the authors encouraged all of those involved in the action research—teachers, teacher-leaders, principals, and graduate students—to individually and collectively reflect on the action research and its effects. This book has given all of us an opportunity to practice what we preach—to reflect on our own roles as facilitators of collaborative action research as well as the action research itself as it played out differently in different schools.

This book is divided into two parts. In the Introduction, preceding Part I, I define collaborative action research, describe the research process, and discuss the integrative power of collaborative action research. I also introduce Texas State University's School Improvement Network, its principles and goals, and the support it provided to Network schools engaged in school-wide action research.

Part I focuses on the University's role in collaborative action research, although the reader will quickly find that we cannot explore the experiences of professors and graduate students involved in collaborative research without also exploring the experiences of their practitioner partners. Chapter 1 tells the story of Miguel Guajardo's work with school practitioners, graduate students, and community members in the early stages of collaborative action research. Miguel presents a change process concept map developed by his students out of their work with a Network school. Sarah Nelson describes in Chapter 2 her service as a critical friend. She stresses the need for a critical friend to establish credibility, negotiate multiple relationships, and to both support and challenge the partner school. Charles Slater, in Chapter 3, reviews a variety of ways in which his graduate students were involved with action research in Network schools, and describes what his students learned from their work with the schools. Charles then expands the concept of collaborative action research to the international level, sharing his experiences working with graduate students in Mexico. In Chapter 4, John Smyth urges universities to increase their involvement in collaborative action research. John presents five propositions central to the advancement of universities' engagement in collaborative research.

Part II is concerned primarily with schools' experiences with collaborative action research; however, as in Part I, you will find that the school and university sides of collaborative action research cannot really be separated. Chapter 5, authored by Gordon, Stiegelbauer, and Diehl, describes characteristics of more and less successful action research programs at Network schools. The schools with more successful programs were classified as *high performance schools,* and the less successful schools were classified as either *coasters* or *wheel spinners.* Marla McGhee and Michael Boone's Chapter 6 addresses the concept of readiness for collaborative action research. Marla and Mike identify attributes of schools ready and not ready for action research and school improvement, with an emphasis on challenges faced by high schools. These authors also discuss how schools not ready for action research and school improvement can move toward readiness.

In Chapter 7, Suzanne Stiegelbauer provides a comprehensive discussion of a critical but often neglected aspect of collaborative action research: implementation. Suzanne examines the different dimensions of implementation and offers practical guidelines for successful implementation. Jane Ross writes in Chapter 8 of a Network school's action research to improve school culture and climate. Jane illustrates the inherent relationship of action research with school culture and climate, and shows us that in some schools improving school culture and climate goes hand in hand with improving student achievement. In Chapter 9, Barbara Davis and Iris Escandón relate the story of action research in a school that joined the School Improvement Network in the school's first year of operation. This school used peer coaching to both build community and improve reading achievement in its first year, and expanded action research to other content areas in its second year.

The Conclusion consolidates what those of us associated with the School Improvement Network have learned from our work with the Network into sets of suggestions for universities and schools.

Collaborative action research is hard work for everyone involved— teachers, principals, professors, and graduate students—and even with all of the hard work there is no guarantee of success. Adequate internal and external support, however, greatly increases the likelihood of success, and success at collaborative action research can transform participants into reflective inquirers and schools into communities of inquiry. Most importantly, collaborative action research can transform student learning.

Acknowledgments

ALL OF THE AUTHORS in this book must be acknowledged not only for their contributions to the book but also for the work they did with school leaders and teachers during the action research projects the book is based on. At most universities there are a few faculty members who are willing to devote considerable time and energy to working with public school practitioners to improve teaching and learning in schools, despite the fact that there is little or no extrinsic reward for such services. They do this because of their commitment to public education, to educators, and to children. The authors whose work you are about to read belong in this category. It is with a deep sense of respect and appreciation that I introduce their stories and reflections to you.

The school administrators, teacher-leaders, and other teachers who carried out the action research for school improvement this book reports on also need to be acknowledged as belonging to a special group of educators. In this age of mandated curriculum, scripted lessons, and high-stakes tests, it takes courage to initiate school improvement focused on local needs, teacher inquiry, and collaborative action, and to share student learning data, instructional problems, and research results with practitioners from other schools and university professors. Some of the action research projects described in this book were more successful than others, but all of the practitioners who participated in the projects deserve to be recognized for their efforts to improve student learning.

I take this opportunity to acknowledge John Beck, professor emeritus and former dean of the College of Education at Texas State University, who helped to procure funding for the National Center for School Improvement (NCSI) and the School Improvement Network, and who provided moral as well as material support for our work with schools. Marla McGhee, although she was coordinating the innovative Principals Preparation Partnership—the "other side" of NCSI—performed double duty by assisting the School Improvement Network whenever she was asked to do so.

Finally, many thanks to doctoral student and graduate assistant Erin Ali Ronder, who helped me with the myriad tasks associated with editing this book and kept a good sense of humor throughout.

—Stephen P. Gordon

The Power of Collaborative Action Research

Stephen P. Gordon

Steve Gordon coordinated the School Improvement Network.

COLLABORATIVE ACTION RESEARCH, when it works as intended, can empower educators, transform school cultures, and most importantly, dramatically improve student learning. What, then, *is* collaborative action research and why is it so powerful? Sagor (2000) defines action research as "a disciplined process of inquiry conducted by and for those taking the action" (p. 4). Calhoun (2002) defines action research as "continued disciplined inquiry conducted to inform and improve our practice as educators" (p. 18). Action research can be done by individual educators, small groups of educators, or schoolwide. Tillotson (2000) describes schoolwide action research:

> Teachers or administrators focus on a specific, significant problem in the school. The action researchers ask questions about the problem, develop a plan for gathering informative data, and carefully analyze the data to make the most informed choices about how to resolve the issue. (p. 31)

Some authors describe *collaborative* action research as a university professor or other outside researcher doing action research with a small group of teachers, thus distinguishing it from research by individual teachers or schoolwide research. This book takes the position that university professors or other outside experts can engage in collaborative action research on any level—with individual teachers, with small groups, or schoolwide. Indeed, we argue that *schoolwide* collaborative action research is the most powerful type of collaborative research because of its potential for bringing about

1

whole-school improvement. The focus of this book, then, is on university–school collaboration to facilitate schoolwide action research.

The schoolwide action research process is simple enough to diagram (see Figure I.1). The school community gathers and analyzes preliminary data for the purpose of selecting a focus area, then gathers target data to better understand the focus area and how to plan for change. Based on its analysis of target data, the school prepares a long-term action plan. The school implements the action plan, gathers evaluation data to assess the plan's implementation and effects, and revises the plan accordingly. The process is not intended to yield generalizable results, but to solve practical problems identified by the school community. In *collaborative* schoolwide action research, university professors (and sometimes their graduate students) or other outside experts assist the school with each phase of the action research. When universities sponsor regional networks of schools engaged in action research, a new dimension is added: the collaboration of schools within the network as they assist each other through the action research process.

Although the research process is the most obvious characteristic of action research, a strong argument can be made that the *integrative nature* of action research is what makes it such a powerful vehicle for school improvement. *Collaborative* action research can be even more integrative—and even more powerful. Next I will discuss the elements of school improvement that are integrated in schoolwide collaborative action research.

THE INTEGRATIVE POWER OF COLLABORATIVE ACTION RESEARCH

Collaborative action research for school improvement integrates research with action, action with reflection, critique with collaboration, research with democracy, empowerment with accountability, teacher development with school development, schools with universities, and schools with a larger professional learning community. Although all of these elements interact with each other in synergy, for the purpose of discussion I will examine dyads of interacting elements.

Research with Action

Collaborative action research integrates research and action in a number of ways that traditional research does not. First, action research integrates the investigation of problems with the solving of those problems. Second, in action research the researchers and the action-takers are the same. This means that those who best know the learners and the educational environment can

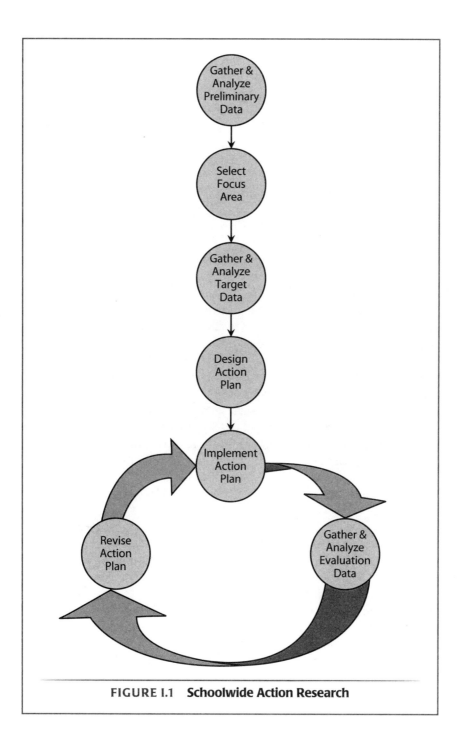

FIGURE I.1   Schoolwide Action Research

embed their knowledge and concerns in the research, and play the central role in deciding the implications of the research for action. Third, the research and action take place in the same context, meaning that the research can directly inform and validate action (Crawford & Cornett, 2000).

Not all of the research in action research needs to be generated locally. Outside research can provide valuable knowledge that informs local action. Calhoun suggests integrating internal and external research in the action planning process. A long-range goal of action research is to establish inquiring communities that continuously use internal and external research to inform and assess action (Calhoun, 2002).

Action with Reflection

Reason (2004) remarks on the dynamic nature of action research: "Action research is a process that grows, develops, shifts, changes over time . . . the questions, relationships, and purposes may change; what is seen as important may change" (p. 273). Reason goes on to explain that it is the iterative process of action and reflection that makes action research so dynamic. Reflection on action informs and improves future action.

Systematically reflecting on one's performance at each stage of the problem-solving process enables more effective problem-solving (Moss, 1997). When teachers are provided time and opportunity to reflect on teaching and learning in general and on their own teaching in particular, they develop a better understanding of exemplary teaching (National Research Council, 1996). Just as reflection on teaching enhances teaching and learning in the classroom, so reflection on collective action enhances the school improvement process.

The integration of reflection and action in schoolwide action research means that educators reflect on each phase of action research, including:

- Reflection on the data gathering and data analysis process as well as the data themselves
- Reflection on decision-making regarding selection of the focus area as well as the focus area
- Reflection on the action planning process as well as the action plan
- Reflection on each phase of the action plan's implementation
- Reflection on the process of evaluating the action research as well as the results of the evaluation
- Reflection on the process of revising the action plan as well as the revised plan
- Ongoing reflection on the school's development as a community of inquiry

The iterative process of action and reflection has short-range and long-range purposes. The short-range purpose is to improve the quality of the action research and its effects. The long-range purpose is to develop the school as a community of inquiry.

Critique with Collaboration

Educators involved in action research collaborate to critique and improve practice. In a seminal study of successful and unsuccessful schools, Little (1982) found that critique and collaboration intersected in the successful schools:

- Teachers engage in frequent, continuous, and increasingly concrete and precise talk about teaching practice.
- Teachers are frequently observed and provided with useful (if potentially frightening) critiques of their teaching.
- Teachers plan, design, research, evaluate, and prepare teaching materials together.
- Teachers teach each other the practice of teaching. (p. 331)

Wasley, Hampel, and Clark (1997) found that critical feedback from external partners as well as self-critique broadened and deepened whole-school improvement efforts. Wasley et al. recommend that schools investigate their progress through a combination of civil discourse (extended, thoughtful dialogue characterized by mutual respect) and rigorous analysis (critical examination of improvement efforts in light of students' learning).

In collaborative action research, critique and collaboration merge. Members of the school community collaborate with each other and with university partners for data-based critique of current practice, to improve school practice, and to critique improvement efforts. Because much of schoolwide action research is implemented in classrooms, critique and collaboration at the school and classroom levels tend to merge. For example, if the school is implementing inquiry learning as part of its action research, teachers will need to observe and critique each other trying out inquiry-based lessons. Teachers involved in collective improvement efforts are less likely to cling to the norm of privacy found in conventional schools, and are more likely to become open to critique of their teaching as well as collaborative efforts to improve teaching.

Research with Democracy

Allen and Calhoun (1998) warn that "action research cannot be viewed as an effort that is separate from a school's governance" (p. 710). The data-based inquiry, reflection, critique, and collaboration that characterize action research require a democratic environment. Conversely, action research is a tailor-made tool for democratic change.

Integration of research and democracy requires more than the school simply taking a vote on the direction in which it wishes to proceed on action research. Democratic discussion is a necessity, and this in turn requires small groups meeting on a regular basis. The League of Professional Schools recommends randomly assigning each professional in the school to a liaison group. Liaison groups discuss school improvement needs and ideas for action, and their representatives take recommendations to an executive committee that uses a democratic process to consider proposals (Glickman, Gordon, & Ross-Gordon, 2007). Some schools alternate between small-group and whole-school meetings: The small groups allow in-depth discussion and high levels of participation, and the whole-school meetings allow for sharing among groups and schoolwide decision-making on important issues.

Policies and procedures must be established for democratic participation in action research. Some schools establish a policy that all professionals in the school may participate in decision-making. Other schools include parent and community representatives with voting power in decision-making groups. Some schools require a simple majority on decisions regarding action research; others require a two-thirds or even an 85% majority on major decisions.

Although the particular policies and procedures for decision-making may vary from school to school, it is important that democratic decision-making be used to answer each of several questions during the action research process:

1. What types of preliminary data should we gather, and what methods should we use to gather them?
2. What should be our focus area for action research?
3. What types of target data should be gathered, and what methods should we use to gather them?
4. What should be our action research objectives?
5. What activities should we carry out to reach our objectives?
6. What types of evaluation data should we gather to determine the effects of our action research, and what methods should we use to gather them?
7. How should we revise our action research?

Democratic decision-making to answer each of these questions, of course, needs to be informed decision-making—informed by external research and by knowledge gained during the previous phases of action research.

Empowerment with Accountability

Attending an action research network meeting or visiting a school where action research is going well, one cannot help but notice the sense of empowerment among administrators and teachers. Educators in communities of inquiry still have to deal with high-stakes testing and central office mandates, but the school community also is involved in its own exciting initiative, which *it* controls and which it typically considers far more relevant to the improvement of student learning than external mandates. At the root of empowerment is the creation of new knowledge, new abilities, and new capacities. "Action research is emancipatory; it leads not just to new practical knowledge, but to new abilities to create knowledge" (Reason & Bradbury, 2001, p. 2). Action research builds the school's problem-solving capacity (Hughes, 2003) and empowers the school to create change (Gardner, 2004).

Teachers and principals empowered by action research tend to lose their fear of external accountability as they begin to focus on internal accountability. Teachers in a study by Raptis and Fleming (2005) reported that their participation in action research "helped them implement a change of culture and helped them realize, as teachers, they could guide their own professional growth through research, reflection, and improvements to instructional practice" (para. 36). Calhoun (2002) explains that action research can change a school's culture so that continuous, data-based assessment and professional growth are both accepted and supported. An assistant principal participating in collaborative action research illustrates Calhoun's point:

> As a contemporary administrator, I want to make informed decisions based on both qualitative and quantitative information that can show how learning has been affected by our efforts. I use action research, formally and informally, to gather the data I need. I have internalized the process of data gathering through action research so that I can make administrative decisions based on sound knowledge rather than on my best guess. Now, I cannot even think about school improvement without planning to obtain the data we will need to make decisions. (McLaughlin, Watts, & Beard, 2000, p. 290)

Action research empowers teachers, principals, and school communities to place externally imposed accountability into perspective, to envelop external accountability measures within more balanced and more meaningful assessments of school improvement and student learning, and to shift toward an emphasis on self-accountability.

Teacher Development with School Development

Schoolwide action research integrates the development of individual teachers and small groups of teachers with whole-school improvement. Schoolwide data gathering and analysis, goal setting, and action planning invariably lead to smaller groups and individuals implementing a great deal of the improvement efforts that follow. Grade-level teams, content-area teams, interdisciplinary teams, and many other small groups experience their own professional development as they contribute to the larger action research effort. Beyond the general benefits of professional inquiry, many processes associated with teacher development typically are integrated in the implementation phase of action research. Training programs, collegial support groups, peer coaching, reflective writing, and teacher leadership are a few examples of teacher development processes that often are integrated with action plans.

Successful action research ultimately has its greatest impact in the classroom, the primary focus of teaching and learning. Through collaborating in action research, individual teachers can develop cognitively and pedagogically and, according to many teachers involved in action research, rejuvenate their professional careers. The ultimate goal of action research is to develop a community of inquiry, but we should not forget that a community of inquiry is made up of inquiring groups and individuals.

Schools with Universities

The integration of school and university efforts in collaborative action research offers advantages to both parties. Allen and Calhoun (1998) found that schools with the most technical support and professional development were the most successful with action research, and the university is a natural provider of such assistance. The university can share with the school a body of research and theory on both the action research process and the school's particular focus area. Professors can help the school select or design data gathering tools and assist with data analysis. University partners can provide the school with critical feedback during each phase of the action research process. One of the most important things the university can do for the school is to provide moral support. Raptis and Fleming (2005) stress the importance of helping school staffs "to overcome their fears about research methods, their concerns about the evidence they collected, and the value of what they deemed important" (para. 30).

Universities and professors also have much to gain from participating in PK–12 action research. Working with schools helps the university to fulfill its service mission and to develop positive relationships with communities and schools. Professors can do research *on* school action research and publish the results. Collaborative action research provides professors with, in Tillotson's (2000) words, "a dose of practical reality concerning school-based issues" (p. 33). Involvement in school-based research thus can inform professors' teaching and make it more relevant. Also, schools engaged in collaborative action research can serve as learning laboratories for graduate students, who can experience the research process first hand as they assist practitioners with reviews of literature, data gathering, and data analysis.

Of course, there are risks associated with collaborative research. Professors must keep in mind that the primary research is the school's, not the professor's. The school's view of the best action research design may not be the same as the professor's, and the professor needs to balance the need for a rigorous design with the goal of empowerment (Raptis & Fleming, 2005). Through ongoing dialogue, school practitioners and university professors need to establish a collaborative agenda (Reason, 2004). Successful collaborative action research is characterized by mutual adaptation of school and university schemas of action research.

Schools with a Larger Professional Learning Community

Action research networks, often sponsored and coordinated by universities, give schools engaged in action research an opportunity to become part of a larger professional learning community. Although the focus of collaborative action research is the individual school, action research leadership teams from network schools often meet together at the university that coordinates the network. Network meetings typically include professional development sessions on the action research process. These sessions usually provide opportunities for leadership teams from different schools to share data, plans, feedback, problems, and possible solutions. As the action research proceeds, "a large professional learning community provides a real audience and purpose for sharing results and promising practices" (Halbert & Kaser, 2002, p. 19).

Just as schoolwide action research provides a "cause beyond oneself" for teachers (Glickman et al., 2007), so membership in an action research network provides a cause and community beyond one's school. Although a school district can create its own internal network, regional networks tend to allow for more freedom of expression, more diversity, and more creative thinking. Administrators and teachers serving on action research leadership teams often discuss the value of getting away from the busy routines and daily stress of their schools and districts, and report that network meetings allow them to focus on the "big picture" of school improvement and relate that big picture to their school's action research. Working with teams from other districts exposes leadership teams to a wide range of experiences, ideas, and expertise.

There are a number of regional action research networks around the nation. Examples include the League of Professional Schools, coordinated by the University of Georgia, and the League of Education Action Researchers in the Northwest (Project Learn), coordinated by Washington State University. An action research network that I was associated with for several years—The School Improvement Network—is described below.

HARNESSING THE POWER OF ACTION RESEARCH: THE SCHOOL IMPROVEMENT NETWORK

The School Improvement Network, sponsored by the National Center for School Improvement at Texas State University, was developed around the principles and goals listed in Figure I.2. Schools interested in joining the Network attended an orientation at which they were presented the Network's principles and goals, an overview of the Network's action research process, and a summary of benefits and responsibilities of Network membership. Schools wishing to join the Network then committed to at least one year of Network membership.

Each school in the Network selected an action research leadership team consisting of the principal, at least three teachers, and one other member of the school community. The purpose of the leadership team was to facilitate the entire school community in schoolwide action research. The Network provided day-long workshops for leadership teams, spaced out across two academic years. Initial workshops focused on training in the action research process and included topics like shared governance, the action research cycle, data gathering, data analysis, selection of a focus area, and action planning. As schools become engaged in action research, training shifted to implementation, evaluation, and revision of action research. Each workshop included opportunities for leadership teams from different schools to discuss new knowledge and skills and to share ideas for applying new learning. Each workshop also gave leadership teams time for planning how they would facilitate the next phase of action research in their school. Eventually, leadership teams brought data, action plans, and results to share, and received feedback on their action research from university professors and other leadership teams.

The Network assigned a *critical friend* to each Network school to provide the school with technical and moral support throughout the action research

National Center for School Improvement (NCSI)
School Improvement Network

Principles

1. School improvement is continuous renewal, not a single reform or event.
2. Inquiry as a habit of mind is essential to school improvement. Inquiry means questioning current practices and seeking research-based ideas about improvements to be made.
3. Vision building, curriculum development, professional development, and action research are core strategies for improving schools, teaching, and learning. Classroom observation and feedback, visits to others' classrooms, study groups, systematic data collection, and assistance from critical friends all can contribute to the improvement process.
4. All individuals in the school organization need to learn, to teach, and to lead. Formal leaders must be facilitators able to stimulate and develop the abilities of educators, parents, and students.

Goals

1. Create new models of school leadership and teacher leadership to develop the wise, competent, and caring educators needed to lead school improvement efforts.
2. Reclaim the public purpose of education and democracy by ensuring that school improvement efforts are linked tightly to promoting students as valued and valuable citizens.
3. Provide professional development and technical assistance to school leadership teams (including principals and teachers) charged with coordinating school improvement projects.
4. Focus school improvement efforts on the improved academic achievement of all students, and on reducing the achievement gap among various groups of students.
5. Improve the performance of schools in high need areas.
6. Identify successful school improvement models, and disseminate nationally information on those models.

FIGURE I.2   Network Principles and Goals

process. Critical friends were either professors or advanced doctoral students majoring in school improvement. All doctoral students serving as critical friends had considerable experience as educational leaders. Critical friends were asked to visit their assigned schools regularly and assist with developing data gathering instruments, analyzing data, action planning, implementation, and so on.

Network schools were provided some financial assistance by the Network. Workshops and critical friends were provided at no cost, and the Network covered the cost of release time for teachers on leadership teams to attend Network meetings. Each year, $1,000 mini-grants were given to Network schools to assist with their action research. Additional $500 mini-grants were provided to schools for development of school portfolios to document the action research and its results. Finally, the university paid stipends to university professors who delivered on-site workshops focused on schools' particular action research efforts.

Other Network assistance was provided on an individual basis as requested. For example, university graduate classes in partnership with the Network provided some schools with reviews of literature on their action research focus areas. Other graduate classes assisted schools with data gathering and data analysis. Graduate students who provided assistance to Network schools did so as part of their course requirements for classes like School as the Center of Inquiry, Continuous School Improvement, and Models of Educational Assessment.

After two years of action research, Network schools were invited to share their research at a regional conference sponsored by the Network. Educators from throughout Central Texas attended the conference, which gave Network schools the opportunity to share results with educators from outside the Network, be publicly recognized for their school improvement efforts, and celebrate their progress.

Not all of the Network schools experienced success with action research, and those that did experienced different levels of success. Chapter 5 reports on a study that examines Network schools' action research efforts and results, and the other chapters in this book draw heavily on case studies on action research at Network schools.

PART I

The University's Role

CHAPTER 1

Developing Partnership

The Early Stages of Collaborative Action Research

Miguel A. Guajardo

Miguel Guajardo served as a critical friend to a School Improvement Network school and taught graduate classes that partnered with the school.

I ASPIRE THAT THE WORK I do as a teacher, researcher, and community builder will have a transformational impact. I might not always transform my partners, but I change every time I engage in collaborative inquiry. My background includes extensive work in school and community development, focused on fostering students' intellectual and social development through an exploration of self and community. This has included working with teachers to develop culturally relevant pedagogy and working with teachers and parents to develop students as leaders who take responsibility for their community (Guajardo, 2002; Guajardo & Guajardo, 2002; Guajardo, Guajardo, & Casaperalta, 2008). It was with this background that I joined the faculty in Educational Leadership at Texas State University and began my work with the School Improvement Network.

As a critical friend I was asked to work with San Joaquin High School, a school with a majority Latino population. The first year of the partnership was spent developing a relationship with members of the school community, gathering and analyzing preliminary (needs assessment) data, developing an action research model to assist San Joaquin through the school improvement process, completing reviews of literature to inform the school's action research, and developing discussion questions intended to foster dialogue about school improvement within the San Joaquin community. This chapter will focus on that first year of partnership. One of my goals as a critical friend was to involve my graduate students as much as possible in the start-up phase of collaborative action research. Students in the course

School as the Center of Inquiry worked with San Joaquin in the fall and spring, and students in the class Campus Leadership worked with the school during the summer.

STAGE 1: BUILDING RELATIONSHIPS

My invitation to participate as a critical friend was followed by a visit with the high school's dean of instruction. I quickly found out that I was not the only new person in town; almost the entire administration was also new. The only administrator with local experience was an assistant principal. We agreed that the school and I could be a good match; the administration valued my experience working in Latino communities.

The initial meeting hosted by the Network was in a traditional conference setting. We talked to the conference participants about the background of the Center and its history, accomplishments, and expectations. People introduced themselves and their schools. The first activity was a table conversation in which each administrator and teacher talked about his or her own expectations. During these introductions, it occurred to me that the teachers from San Joaquin I was working with did not even know each other. And they certainly didn't know what the Network initiative was about. The situation was that San Joaquin's action research leadership team had been reconfigured, and everyone from San Joaquin at the conference—including administrators and teachers—was new to the team and had not been involved in the school's orientation to the Network.

At that moment I stopped what was superficial conversation and caucused with the group. The question posed to the participants at the table was "Is this the agenda we need for our team?" The resounding response was "No!" At that point, we removed ourselves from the conference and went to sit alone in a corner of the building. It was clear to me that we needed some community-building within the group if we were to accomplish anything the first year. At this point we began to share stories, interests, strengths, and concerns. The team began to buy into the community-building process when two veteran teachers found out that even though they had worked together for years, they didn't know they had grown up in the same East Texas town and had lived several blocks from each other in their hometown. If this was a mystery, what else had the teachers failed to learn about each other because of their isolation? The story sharing process was powerful, and at the end of a two-hour conversation we agreed that this collaborative initiative was important and worthwhile.

After the Network meeting we continued to meet with each other and work on our relationships and roles. I made frequent visits to campus, visiting with teachers, administrators, and community people. These conversations were critically important in creating readiness and negotiating entry for my students and me. Late in the fall semester I agreed to do a staff development session with the whole school. I invited several of my students from the course School as the Center of Inquiry, and they became part of the inquiry process.

STAGE 2: BRINGING THE PARTNERS TOGETHER

Graduate students were invited to join me at a whole-school session at San Joaquin, followed by a smaller work session with the action research leadership team and the graduate students. The purpose of the whole-school session was to introduce the concept of schoolwide collaborative action research to the entire school community. In a presentation to the administrators, faculty, staff, and graduate students, I stressed the benefits of collaborative action research for students, families, teachers, staff, and the community. To establish credibility with the group, I discussed my 15 years of school community research and the positive effects of that research on student academic success and community development. I described the challenges of marginalized children who come to a school that is culturally incongruent with the world they live in. I discussed the need for teachers to align the world of school with the world students come from, to be advocates for their students, to help children and families build hope for the future, and to assume responsibility for helping children and families reach their dreams. The whole-school session concluded with a video in which four minority students shared their stories of identity, struggle, and personal growth.

Following the whole-school session, the graduate students, the school's action research leadership team (including several teachers), and I met to debrief the session and to discuss school issues and needs. We discussed disengagement of some teachers during the whole-school session, as indicated by their body language and the fact that they were chatting with each other rather than attending to session activities.

Our discussion turned to the demographics of the school. Three of the four school administrators were White. Eighty percent of the faculty was White. The student population, in contrast, was 63% Hispanic, 31% White, and 5% African American. Another discussion topic was the repeated changes the school had experienced over the past several years, with several different administrators and academic programs coming and going. We agreed on a broad question that preliminary data gathering would address: "How do we build a foundation for a positive relationship among the diverse groups in the San Joaquin High School community that will lead to sustainable school improvement efforts?" We decided to gather preliminary data that would both address this broad question and identify specific school needs.

STAGE 3: GATHERING AND ANALYZING PRELIMINARY DATA

A new group of graduate students in the spring class School as the Center of Inquiry collaborated with San Joaquin's teachers in preliminary data gathering. After I shared information about the fall's work at San Joaquin with the graduate students, they collaborated with teachers and administrators at the high school to design a needs assessment that would gather data from students, teachers, administrators, community members, and archival sources. Specific data gathering methods included

- Questionnaires
- Observations
- Oral histories
- Interviews
- Analysis of existing data such as historical documents, previously administered questionnaires, student achievement data, and demographic data on the school and community

Some of the more interesting findings from the preliminary needs assessment are discussed here.

Educational History of San Joaquin

Stories of the community history were developed through archival data from the public library and through personal stories of citizens gathered through an oral history process. These stories were enlightening to many members of the school community. For example, many students, teachers, and parents were not aware that students in San Joaquin had once been segregated in African American, Mexican, and White schools. Recent history also was documented. For instance, many members of the community were very disappointed that there had been no Cinco de Mayo celebration in the community that year for the first time in memory. The educational history of San Joaquin provided a context in which to examine the high school's present issues and concerns.

Teachers' Perceptions

The faculty was concerned with the "revolving door" of school administrators. Teachers had seen administrators come and go, and believed teachers had been the ones keeping the system going. One teacher stated, "In the corporate world, we call this a hostile takeover. A new administration comes in and nobody asks us what we want or need." The lack of teacher involvement in decision-making had created teacher resentment and a perceived lack of respect for teachers. Teachers reported that, not only were they not consulted on changes, information about changes was not getting to them. An "us versus them" mentality had developed.

Academically, the greatest teacher concern was the high rate of failure at the ninth-grade level. Many students were in their second year of ninth grade. A ninth-grade learning center had been established to deal with the problem, but the center's effectiveness had yet to be assessed.

Student Perceptions

A schoolwide student questionnaire was administered, and focus groups were held with students from different grade levels and ethnic groups. Students reported a lack of pride in the school. Many of the students with older brothers and sisters had developed expectations based on stories shared by their siblings (stories of "pride days," "color days," painting the school and their classrooms, and so on). However, current students' experiences had been very different from those of their older siblings and had been disappointing.

The school had been awarded a Pregnancy and Parenting Grant (PEP), and a Casa Esperanza grant from the local university also provided school services. There was a child-care center, and drug and alcohol counseling was provided. Highly capable professionals were delivering these services; however, the services were disconnected and fragmented. There was no system for coordinating referrals or services. The coordinators of the social service programs had not effectively shared information about the services; thus, the school administration had resisted referring students. The issue was not a lack of quality, but a lack of communication leading to a lack of understanding and trust.

Needs Identified

Our analysis of the preliminary data led to the identification of a number of needs for the school to consider as it developed an action plan. These needs included the following:

- A leadership strategy that would help the school community clarify its values, develop a vision for the future based on those values, and agree on a process for moving toward that vision
- An organizational structure that would include parents, teachers, and students in the decision-making process
- A communication system that would enable the sharing of information and allow two-way communication between the administration and teachers and between the school and community
- Staff development that would enable teachers, administrators, and other staff to understand the community's changing demographics and develop the cultural competence to address these changing demographics
- Community outreach that would invite the parents into the school
- A school safety program that would include adults being visible on campus at all times
- Curriculum and instructional changes at the ninth-grade level that would meet the needs of these students and provide individualized assistance to students with academic problems; this need was part of a larger need for schoolwide curriculum improvement

This list of needs was quite daunting to a school trying to organize for action research. Everyone agreed that not all of these needs could be met at once, and that none could be met overnight. What the school needed was a model for prioritizing needs, gathering target data on its most important needs, and developing an action plan to meet priority needs. Although an action research model would be an important source of assistance, San Joaquin would need other types of support to initiate the action research process. Research on areas related to San Joaquin's identified needs, especially research on leadership for school improvement, would assist teachers and administrators planning action research for school improvement. Dialogue is a cornerstone of school improvement, and questions formulated by doctoral students would provide a basis for such dialogue. These types of support were provided in Stage 4.

STAGE 4: SUPPORT FOR ACTION PLANNING

The philosophy of the School Improvement Network is that Network schools identify their own school improvement goals and develop their own action plans for achieving those goals. In line with this philosophy, graduate students in the summer course Campus Leadership and I focused on providing support for San Joaquin's action planning process. First, the graduate students reviewed the preliminary data gathered in the spring in order to familiarize themselves with the high school and its needs. Next, we developed an action research model. That was consistent with the needs identified from the preliminary data and provided a structure for moving forward, but it left key decisions in the hands of the school community. Leadership (by administrators, teachers, and parents) would be an important part of action research at San Joaquin, so the students completed and summarized reviews of literature on different aspects of leadership to be shared with the high school. Administrators and teachers would need not only to review the literature on leadership but also to discuss how to apply concepts in the literature to their own school improvement efforts, so the graduate students also prepared discussion questions to spark dialogue within the school community. Next I will take a closer look at each form of assistance that was provided at this stage.

The Action Research Model

We developed a seven-step action research model for use by San Joaquin that would leave all key decisions in the hands of the high school. The model is shown in Figure 1.1.

The first step in the model was to form a development team that would include but extend beyond the action research leadership team, including representatives of all stakeholder groups. The second step would consist of discussion among members of the development team. Input for discussion would include the needs identified from the preliminary data, the review of literature on leadership, and the discussion questions developed by the graduate students. The discussion in Step 2 would lead to Step 3: writing of beliefs and values statements, and identification of a broad focus area and school improvement goals.

Step 4 would consist of gathering and analyzing target data on the focus area. The target data would include a second review of literature by graduate students covering the school's specific focus for school improve-

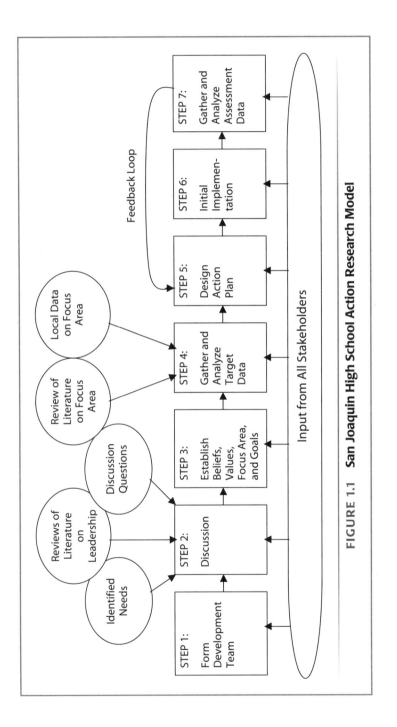

FIGURE 1.1   San Joaquin High School Action Research Model

ment. Other target data would be data gathered at the high school and in the community. The target data would inform Step 5: development of an action plan. Step 6 would be the initial implementation of the action plan. Step 7 would consist of gathering and analyzing data to assess the progress of the action plan's implementation and early effects, and would provide feedback for any necessary revision of the action plan before continued implementation. At each stage, the development team would seek input from all stakeholders before making decisions relevant to that stage. The action research model gave San Joaquin a generic map to follow through the process, but also gave the schoolwide latitude in pursuing its own improvement efforts.

Reviews of the Literature

We provided the school with brief reviews of literature on school leadership as input to the discussion in Step 2 of the action research model. Teams of graduate students completed reviews on organizational leadership, instructional leadership, and school and community leadership. An example of a brief review of the literature—the review on school and community leadership—is provided in the Appendix. For each review of literature, we also provided the high school with the original literature and an annotated bibliography on the topic reviewed.

Discussion Questions

To help the school community initiate discussions on school leadership in Step 2 of the action research model, we designed sets of discussion questions on each of the aforementioned areas of leadership: organizational leadership, instructional leadership, and school and community leadership. The questions are listed here:

For Organizational Leadership

1. What is the vision of your school?
2. What values drive this school?
3. How do students, families, teachers, parents, and the community feel connected to the school?
4. How are the students, teachers, and parents empowered at school?
5. What are the expectations of students, teachers, parents, and community partners at your school?

For Instructional Leadership

1. What programs are currently in place to enhance student preparedness for higher education? Are the programs effective? Why or why not?
2. What curriculum and instructional strategies are currently used to enhance culturally responsive instruction?
3. What research has been performed to find data from successful schools with similar demographics?
4. What current systems are in place to communicate instructional expectations?

For School and Community Leadership

1. What is the dominant paradigm of school/community relations? How does it benefit students? Staff? Parents? Is it the most effective model for this community?
2. What structures are currently in place that either inhibit or promote communication of curriculum expectations and other information between families and school? Do the parents and students know what it takes to get into college?
3. Knowing that a student's life outside of school affects how well he or she will do in school, what strategies and attitudes can teachers and administrators adopt to recognize what families bring to the process of educating students? How can the school promote cultural competence for the staff, students, and community?
4. What structures and practices promote the building of social capital in the school community?

The graduate students and I presented the action research model, reviews of literature, and discussion questions during an interactive session at the high school. San Joaquin's educators welcomed the ideals, process, and information laid out by the graduate students.

CONCLUSION

The early stages of partnership and action research provided advantages for both the school and the graduate students. The school now had data needed to plan for action research, tools to organize for action research, and a map to guide it through the process. Graduate students learned about assessing needs and initiating action research by working with a real school. As they provided service to San Joaquin High School, they developed a sense of worth, relevance, and usefulness. The service provided to the school created a sense of good will between the university and community that had not existed previously.

A number of insights were gained from the early stages of our partnership with San Joaquin High School:

1. University professors and graduate students need to develop personal relationships with school practitioners. Moreover, often the relationships among and between teachers, administrators, parents, and the community need to be improved if the action research is to have a good chance of success.
2. Although practitioners may not have the time to conduct reviews of the literature to inform their action research, they appreciate and use literature reviews completed by their university partners.
3. Practitioners appreciate being provided a general model of what their action research might look like, while maintaining the responsibility for decisions to be made at particular points along the map.
4. An early component of any action research should be an examination of school values, beliefs, and goals; these will form the foundation of successful action research.
5. It is necessary to attend to matters of cultural awareness and cultural competence in action research.
6. Partnership for schoolwide action research needs to extend beyond the university and school and involve the community the school serves.

Even the early stages of partnership and action research, if done well, can be transformational experiences. Although these early stages do not assure success, they can provide the essential foundation for future improvement efforts.

CHAPTER 2

Becoming a Critical Friend

Sarah W. Nelson

Sarah Nelson was a critical friend to a
School Improvement Network school.

THIS CHAPTER TELLS the story of a university faculty member's efforts to serve as a critical friend to a novice principal and a group of teachers in a Network school as they engaged in an action research project to improve literacy learning. The chapter provides a discussion of the critical friend's role in collaborative action research and the challenges and benefits of being a critical friend.

CRITICAL FRIEND DEFINED

External support is frequently cited as a strategy in the school improvement process. In fact, Fullan (2001b) suggests that external involvement is an essential factor in successful school change. Recently, one particular form of external involvement, the critical friend, has gained the attention of practitioners, researchers, and policy-makers (Swaffield, 2004a). For example, the National College for School Leadership (NCSL), a government-sponsored professional development organization in the UK, has endorsed the use of critical friends to help school leaders build confidence in risk-taking and willingness to experiment with new ways of working (National College for School Leadership, n.d.). Similarly, the National School Reform Faculty (NSRF), a professional development initiative originating at the Annenberg Institute of School Reform at Brown University, employs critical friends groups as a means of improving instructional practice among teachers (National School Reform Faculty, n.d.).

In spite of the increasing prevalence of the use of critical friends, there is no accepted definition of the term (Swaffield, 2005). Stenhouse (1975), one of the first to refer to critical friends in the education arena, wrote that critical friends should function as partners to aid teachers as they conduct action research. More recently, Gordon (1999) suggested that critical friends are outsiders who lend their expertise to the school improvement process. Swaffield also discussed the importance of a critical friend as an outsider, and added that the critical friend "not only has a different perspective on the school from those within it, but also assists them to see the familiar with a new light" (p. 45).

Although there is no agreed-upon meaning of the term critical friend, one of the most commonly cited definitions is that given by Costa and Kallick (1993):

> A critical friend . . . is a trusted person who asks provocative questions, provides data to be examined through another lens, and offers critique of a person's work as a friend. A critical friend takes the time to fully understand the context of the work presented and the outcomes that the person or group is working toward. The friend is an advocate for the success of that work. (p. 50)

In this definition, the authors capture the elements that seem to be most central to the concept of critical friend: an outsider position, the ability to see alternative perspectives, a focus on the success of the work, and the trust of those the critical friend serves.

Costa and Kallick (1993) also address an often misunderstood aspect of critical friendship. For many, the words *critical* and *friend* appear to be at odds. How can one be critical and at the same time a friend? Costa and Kallick remind us that although critique often has negative connotations, it is not necessarily so. Critique does not equate to judgment. Rather, critique is an aspect of evaluation, the highest order of thinking on Bloom's taxonomy. Bambino (2002) agrees, stating, "The work is critical because it challenges educators to improve their practice and to bring the changes that the schools need, but the process is neither negative nor threatening" (p. 27). The critical friend relationship can be thought of as one that provides both support and critique in the proper amounts and at the appropriate junctures to keep the work moving forward (MacBeath, 1998; Watling, Hopkins, Harris, & Beresford, 1998).

WHAT DO CRITICAL FRIENDS DO?

As with the definition of the term, the role of the critical friend has been described in many ways. Kember et al. (1997) suggest that the critical friend plays a variety of roles, including financier, rapport builder, mirror, teaching consultant, evaluation advisor, research advisor, and resource provider. Others have metaphorically likened the critical friend to another pair of eyes (Ainscow & Southworth, 1996), a critical ear (MacBeath & Myers, 1999), or an extra pair of hands (National College for School Leadership, n.d.).

Swaffield (2004b), who has written extensively on the subject of critical friendship, helps to define the role of the critical friend by articulating what a critical friend is *not*. According to Swaffield, a critical friend is not an inspector. Inspector implies evaluation, judgment, and imposed agendas, all of which are at odds with critical friendship. The critical friend is also not a counselor. Although a counselor and critical friend may use some of the same skills, counselors are focused on individuals and their feelings; the critical friend is concerned with organizational issues, outcomes, and the effects on all individuals in the organization. Finally, Swaffield asserts that a critical friend is not a coach or mentor. Often coaches and mentors have worked in the same capacity as the person they are coaching or mentoring. This is often not the case for critical friends. Moreover, coaches and mentors "tend to be very directive in their approach, whereas critical friends are more facilitative" (p. 3). For Swaffield, the role most closely linked to critical friend is *consultant*. Even with this term, however, Swaffield notes important differences. For example, she asserts that critical friends tend to be more "process-oriented," "transformative," and engaged in fundamental organizational change, whereas consultants tend to be more "task-oriented," "transactional," and focused on "seeking the solution to a specific problem" (p. 3).

Although the characterizations of critical friends vary, there is agreement about the nature of the work critical friends do. In the main, critical friends offer support to school teams or individual teachers as they implement a change process. Support from the critical friend both reinforces and challenges the work in such a way that the teacher or school team is motivated and empowered to make necessary changes (MacBeath, 1998). In providing support, the critical friend employs multiple strategies, including rapport-building (Kember et al., 1997; Miles, Saxi, & Lieberman, 1988), listening (Swaffield, 2005), observing (NSRF, n.d.; Swaffield, 2004b), questioning (Costa & Kallick, 1993; Gordon, 1999), reflecting (Costa & Kallick, 1993; MacBeath, 1999; Swaffield, 2005), reframing (Schuck & Russell, 2005), providing feedback (Costa & Kallick, 1993; Gordon, 1999; Swaffield, 2005), and mediating conflict (MacBeath, 1999; Miles et al., 1988; Swaffield, 2004b). Additionally, when a critical friend is being used to support school improvement or action research, the critical friend typically brings knowledge and expertise about the change and research processes (McLaughlin & Black-Hawkins, 2004).

Interestingly, although critical friends may bring knowledge and experience related to the area that is the focus of the critical friendship, technical expertise in the focus area is not a necessity for a successful critical friendship. In fact, not knowing about the area of focus may allow the critical friend to ask more powerful questions (Swaffield, 2004a). What *is* necessary is that the critical friend be familiar with the context in which he or she is working. The critical friend will have much more credibility with teachers and school leaders if the critical friend understands the specific environment in which the change effort is occurring (Swaffield, 2004a, 2005) and if the critical friend demonstrates that he or she is "in touch with the realities of school life" (McLaughlin & Black-Hawkins, 2004, p. 280). Having credibility is essential for building a trusting relationship, which is at the heart of a critical friendship (Costa & Kallick, 1993; Kember et al., 1997; McLaughlin & Black-Hawkins, 2004; Swaffield, 2004a, 2005).

MY EXPERIENCE AS A CRITICAL FRIEND

Caulfield is a large elementary school located in the Westview School District. Although it is in a major metropolitan area, the city of Westview is more suburban than urban. Begun in the 1800s as an isolated housing development outside the city limits, Westview grew into an affluent enclave and is today an independent municipality completely surrounded by the larger city. While the metropolitan area is ethnically diverse and has grown increasingly so in recent years, Westview has maintained a population that is more than 90% White and has a poverty rate of less than 4%. The school district is somewhat more diverse because it serves areas outside the town proper. Even so, it is a largely White, affluent district.

Built in 1912, Caulfield is the oldest school in the Westview District. Until the 1950s, the Caulfield campus housed not only an elementary school but also the district's only junior and senior high schools. As a result, many in the community have an affiliation with Caulfield and are vested in its success. This creates a unique environment in which to serve as a school leader. The interest of the community means that Caulfield has access to ample resources. At the same time, the interest of the community means that the principal works under the watchful eye of the town's leaders.

It was in this environment that Amy Sherman began her first year as a principal. Although this was her first principalship, Caulfield was not new to Amy. For the previous two years Amy had served as the school's assistant principal and had been groomed to take over the leadership position after the previous principal announced she would retire. Amy was a somewhat unlikely choice for the position because, although she had worked in the district for nearly a decade, she was not originally from the area, as district employees tended to be. Additionally, Amy was just over 30 years old, much younger than the majority of the faculty. In fact, a number of the teachers remembered having taught Amy's husband when he was a student at Caulfield.

Having spent two years at the school already, Amy knew that changes were needed at Caulfield. As an assistant principal, she had observed in classrooms throughout the school. She found that instruction tended to be didactic and teacher-centered, particularly in the upper grades. The school's achievement data suggested that this approach served some students better than others. While White students, who comprised the majority of the student body, consistently performed well on academic tests, scores for Hispanic students and students living in poverty were significantly lower. Academic reports illustrated that this gap had existed at least since the state initiated an accountability system in the early 1990s, but the gap was becoming a more pressing concern as accountability standards increased. Unless Caulfield addressed the achievement gap, they would lose the high performance rating that was a hallmark of the school.

The issue, however, was bigger than accountability ratings. While nearly everyone at Caulfield was keenly aware that the community expected the school to earn the highest rating, this was not the primary motivation for initiating a change effort. Rather, a number of key people at the school, including the school leaders, seemed to be motivated by an ethical imperative to educate all, not just some, of the students on the campus. This ethical imperative extended not just to getting students to pass accountability tests. School leaders spoke of wanting to improve instruction to actively engage students with learning beyond the basic curriculum. Ironically, in some ways the accountability system had been a hindrance to realizing this vision. Because the school received a high ranking year after year, some faculty members felt little urgency to improve. A reverence for tradition was strongly embedded in the school culture and supported those who were resistant to change. In short, Caulfield was what Stoll and Fink (1998) describe as a cruising school:

> The *cruising school* . . . is perceived as effective, or at least more than satisfactory, by teachers and the school's community. It has a carefully constructed camouflage. While it appears to possess many qualities of an effective school, it is usually located in a more affluent area where pupils achieve in spite of teaching quality. . . . Rankings based on absolute achievement . . . often give the appearance of effectiveness. External per-

ceptions of outside inspectors may also not detect ineffectiveness, and many cruising schools may never be exposed for offering an impoverished diet to their pupils. (p. 193)

Understanding this context, Amy knew change was necessary but would not come easily. Because of this, even before officially taking over the principalship, Amy began to garner external support that would help her move the campus forward.

Joining the School Improvement Network

In the spring before Amy assumed the principalship, Caulfield was invited to participate in an action research network sponsored by the National Center for School Improvement (NCSI) at Texas State University–San Marcos. The purpose of NCSI's School Improvement Network was to provide a forum for university faculty and educational practitioners to work together on school-based collaborative action research teams. The project was structured such that the Network would provide professional development and support over a two-year period so that school leadership teams could learn how to use action research as a tool for school improvement. In turn, the schools agreed to participate in the professional development and to share their experiences with other schools in the Network. After attending an informational meeting, the Caulfield faculty voted to join the Network. A survey of the faculty determined that literacy instruction was the area teachers were most interested in improving. As a result, balanced literacy became the focus of the action research project, and Amy assembled a group of teachers to work with her and the assistant principal to lead the effort.

Forming a Critical Friendship

In the same semester Amy became principal of Caulfield, I joined the faculty of Texas State. I came to Texas State after having served as the principal of a large urban elementary school. The school served a mostly Latino, low-income population, making it quite different from Caulfield. Although the school where I had worked and Caulfield were not alike in terms of the students they served, they shared the challenge of improving literacy learning for all students. As principal, I had spent the better part of seven years leading an action research initiative to develop a strong literacy program. Although we, too, lived with the pressure of the accountability system, our aim was not to raise test scores but rather to raise scholars (O'Neal, Nelson, Gaines,

& Valentino, 2004). We based our improvement efforts on the tenets of valuing student assets, including multiple languages, and developing a love for literacy in all its forms. Because of this experience, the Network coordinator asked me to serve as the critical friend for Caulfield.

Although matching Caulfield and myself made good sense in terms of my knowledge and experience and the school's needs, other factors inhibited the development of a strong critical friendship. As the school year opened, Amy grappled with the myriad tasks it takes to get a school up and running. She was training staff, enrolling students, developing schedules, creating campus plans, and addressing issues and conflicts as they arose. Because she was new to the position, she did not yet have her own systems for accomplishing these tasks. As with many new principals, Amy was consumed with learning to manage and lead the school, leaving little time to focus on a new action research project.

Like Amy, I too was adjusting to a new position. Having just come out of the principalship, where my days unfolded rapidly and my time was not my own, I was learning to live at the university, where the pace is much slower and the work less defined. I did not have people waiting at my office door or dozens of phones calls and e-mails to return as I did when I was a principal. Instead I had course syllabi to develop, textbooks to select and read, papers to grade, research projects to develop, articles to write, and students to advise. Most of these were unfamiliar tasks, and figuring out how to prioritize them and how to work within the organization to accomplish them was new learning for me. Consequently, just as Amy was focused on learning to be a school leader, I was concentrating on becoming a university faculty member and was not fully attentive to my role as critical friend.

Early in the semester I made a few attempts to contact Amy, but when she did not respond, I did not pursue it further. So it was not until midway through the fall semester, when NCSI hosted a workshop for Network schools, that the Caulfield action research team and I finally came together. As we began to introduce ourselves to one another and to discuss how we might go about our work, I discovered that not only were the team members just getting to know me, they were also just getting to know each other. Although Amy had been on the campus for two years, she was in a new role and the teachers were still trying to understand her leadership style. Jon, the assistant principal, was also new to the campus. Like Amy, Jon had come from outside the district, so the teachers did not know him or his style. Of the six teachers on the team, three had joined the faculty only within the last few years. The three veteran teachers on the team had long histories at Caulfield and seemed to know each other well, but not the newer members of the faculty. This lack of familiarity among the team members was a concern. Both collaborative action research and critical friendship depend on collegial, trusting relationships. It was clear that at this point our team lacked these relationships.

The agenda for the Network meeting called for teams to work on developing their action research plans. And while we were eager to formulate a plan, we had no basis for doing so. We agreed that before we could begin to plan, we had to understand where we wanted to go. Moreover, we needed to begin to establish the trusting relationship that is essential for critical friendship (Costa & Kallick, 1993; Kember et al., 1997; McLaughlin & Black-Hawkins, 2004; Swaffield, 2004a, 2005). So we spent the better part of the afternoon learning about one another, what each of us understood about literacy learning, and what we hoped to get out of this project. This proved to be an invaluable investment of our time. The discussion allowed each of us to establish credibility as members of the team and to understand the unique perspective each of us brought.

In discussing her vision for Caulfield, Amy came through as a strong instructional leader. Jon, the assistant principal, displayed a genuine passion for teaching and learning when he talked about his own educational experiences. One of the newer faculty members told how she created a literacy-rich classroom at her previous campus and how this had reignited her joy for teaching. A veteran teacher gave the history of previous efforts to improve literacy learning on the campus and theorized how this might affect the work we wanted to do. For me, the discussion was an opportunity to establish credibility as an academician who not only studied the theory of literacy learning but had also worked to put that theory into practice. As each of us spoke and listened, we began to establish our identity as a team. Because relationships are built over time rather than through a single interaction, it would be an overstatement to say that a critical friendship was formed that day. Yet a foundation for building a relationship had clearly been set. By resisting the urge to jump into action, and instead taking time to learn about one another, we addressed a key aspect successful collaborative relationships—developing connectedness among team members.

In considering each of the team members and the knowledge and experience he or she had to contribute, it became apparent that Amy had been quite astute in selecting the leadership team. Implementing a balanced literacy approach, which emphasizes small-group, differentiated instruction, was going to be a significant change for the school. Whole-class instruction using basal readers and worksheets was the approach favored by many of the Caulfield teachers. A more naive school leader might have created a leadership team comprised only of the small number of teachers, mostly recent hires, who were already using some aspects of the balanced literacy framework. However, despite being a novice leader, Amy had wisely invited teachers with a variety of perspectives to join the team. Some of the teachers she selected were clearly on board and eager to move toward the new model. Other teachers were less enthusiastic, perhaps even resistant, to the idea of large-scale changes to their instructional practice. And while resistance was not something that necessarily benefited the team, the veteran teachers had an important attribute that the other team members did not. As long-term faculty members, they held informal power with other teachers. By inviting them into the process, Amy acknowledged them as leaders and signaled that the project would be an inclusive effort.

In the weeks following the first Network meeting, Amy and I corresponded frequently. As we talked, I gathered information and asked questions to help me better understand the unique context of Caulfield. Additionally, I assisted Amy as she planned a professional development session for the faculty. The purpose of the session was to update the faculty on the work of the leadership team and to provide an overview of the balanced literacy initiative. Although the leadership team had yet to develop an action plan, the team agreed that keeping balanced literacy at the forefront of discussion among the faculty was an important step in maintaining support for the project and would lay the foundation for data gathering. To help with the session, I made arrangements for a colleague who is well known in the literacy field to conduct a workshop for the faculty. The workshop took place in early January when the faculty returned from the winter break. The team reported that the session was well received and that teachers were interested in learning more and wanted to know what the team had planned next.

At our initial meeting, the team agreed that the balanced literacy workshop would be followed by a site visit from a group of educators well versed in balanced literacy. The site visit team would gather baseline data on current literacy practices at Caulfield. As the critical friend, my job was to coordinate the site visit and present the process to the Caulfield faculty. Planning for the site visit was to take place at the January Network meeting. However, due to a last-minute scheduling conflict, no one from the Caulfield leadership team was able to attend that meeting. Without a planning session, we could not proceed with the site visit and data gathering. I was disappointed that the leadership team had not attended the Network meeting, but having worked in schools for many years, I understood how pressing responsibilities can affect campus plans.

Wanting to keep the team on track, I contacted Amy several times over the next few weeks. These contacts, while congenial, did not lead to any further development related to the action research project. The district had unexpectedly initiated a new testing program, and many of the teachers on the leadership team were involved in its implementation. The requirements of the new project made it exceedingly difficult to find a time for the team to meet. Admittedly, I was frustrated. After such a promising start, we seemed to be floundering once again. I worried that the school's commitment to the process was waning, and I was unsure how to respond. I wanted to be respectful of Amy's role as the school leader in determining when the faculty would be ready to resume the action research initiative. Yet, I also feared that if I did not continue to push the project, it would permanently disappear from the school's agenda. Perhaps because I wanted to avoid being seen as a burden more than a support, I opted to step back and wait for the team to let me know when they needed my help. Amy assured me that the team would be at the next Network meeting. With that assurance, I let the next several weeks pass without further contact.

As promised, the entire team attended the next Network meeting. Like our first meeting, this one proved productive and yet also disconcerting for me as a critical friend. As we discussed what had occurred at the school since our last meeting, the team revealed that after the professional development session to introduce balanced literacy, there was much talk among the faculty, and not all of it was positive. Many teachers seemed to be excited about the project and were eager to learn more, but others suggested the campus had been through balanced literacy training and were skeptical of the need for change. Additionally, in an attempt to gain data for the action research project, the team had asked each teacher to complete a self-assessment on guided reading, an aspect of balanced literacy the campus had previously initiated. The assessment responses revealed that while some teachers acknowledged that certain aspects of their literacy instruction could be improved, other teachers indicated they viewed themselves as proficient and not in need of additional professional development in the area of literacy instruction. Because of this dichotomous response, the team was worried that the faculty was beginning to faction, and they were unsure how to respond. Privately, Amy revealed that she was not sure all the team members were on board yet, much less the entire faculty.

As I listened to the team describe what had occurred at the school, I realized that my lack of interaction since the last meeting had been a mistake. I had missed important developments in the team's work. By relying on Amy as the conduit rather than meeting with the team as a whole, I had limited my view of the situation. Perhaps Amy had tried to convey the information to me and I simply did not hear it. Or, perhaps, Amy did not think the incidents significant enough to mention. In any case, it was clear that I had missed an opportunity to be a critical friend to the team.

Feeling as if we had lost time due to my misjudgment, I wanted to help the team regain their momentum. I began to ask clarifying questions about the team's goals and how they might begin to address the faculty's needs. Through this conversation, the team determined that the faculty needed a clearer understanding of the initiative. In general, the faculty appeared to be interested in the project, but they did not know quite what to expect and were unsure of the goals of the action research process and what it meant for their practice. As one teacher indicated, the faculty needed a "vision" of what it meant to use a balanced literacy instructional approach. By giving the faculty a better understanding of balanced literacy and the action research process, the team hoped to unite the campus in support of the initiative.

In addition to a need to better inform the faculty, the team indicated that they needed data to help them understand where the campus stood in terms of literacy instruction. In looking at the action research cycle, the team recognized that although preliminary data had been gathered and analyzed and a focus area had been selected, target data were absent. Each member of the team had anecdotal data to share, but there were no systematically collected data for the team to consider. Without this information, the team was just guessing at what the campus needed. We discussed the site visit and how this could yield important data. A few on the team suggested that a site visit might not be the best approach. With some teachers already having misgivings about the project, experts visiting classrooms might seem like an inspection more than a benign data-gathering activity.

With this perspective, we began to discuss how we could approach the tasks of developing common understanding and gathering data. Initially it was suggested that, because I was affiliated with the Network, it would be appropriate for me to make a presentation to the faculty to explain the project and how action research works and what balanced literacy looks like. Further, since I had experience with data collection, I could lead that process as well. Admittedly, there was a part of me that wanted to do just that. I wanted to make up for having left the team on its own for too long. Yet I knew that this would be another mistake. My role was not to be the expert who comes in to save the day. My role was to help the team develop the knowledge and skills they needed so *they* could lead the initiative. With this in mind, I reframed the conversation to focus on what the team thought the faculty needed to know about the project and about balanced literacy. The team began to generate a list of key ideas. These were then grouped into topic areas, which included an overview of the School Improvement Network and its purpose, an introduction to action research and its benefits, a review of the leadership team's work so far, and a process for developing a vision of the balanced literacy classroom. Using a similar process, we identified data we wanted to collect.

As we looked at the lists, I wondered aloud whether there was a way to present this information as a team rather than having single person do it. One of the team members suggested that we could work in pairs to present each section. To my surprise, Marjorie, one of the veteran teachers who was a seemingly reluctant team member, offered to give an overview of the action research cycle. Following her lead, the other team members volunteered to be responsible for a section. With everyone having a part, we discussed the logistics of the session and developed an agenda. We strategized about how best to engage the faculty and how to ensure that the teachers had ample opportunity to ask questions and provide input. The result was a plan that called for a combination of large-group and small-group discussion and a process that would encourage the faculty to interact with cross-grade-level colleagues. Most importantly, the plan called for each team member to play an active role in facilitating the discussion. Although I was going to provide some background information and help facilitate the process, I was not going to be the *leader* of the session. The team was going to provide leadership collectively. This signaled an important step in the team's development.

Moving Forward

As we began the meeting with the full faculty, there was obvious tension in the room. The crossed arms and defiant looks on the part of some teachers suggested resistance. Others appeared more disinterested than unwilling. And yet, there were a number of teachers who genuinely seemed pleased to be in attendance. So it was in this environment that the team began to talk with the faculty. Marjorie began the discussion. Her presence and leadership had a noticeable effect on the group. The teachers who initially seemed disengaged responded to Marjorie's calls for input. And even as the other team members took the lead, the teachers continued participating. The teachers shared what their vision for Caulfield was and what they understood about good literacy instruction. They talked about the challenges they faced and the strengths of the school. They articulated their concerns and asked questions of the team. As the discussion moved from whole group to small group and back to whole group, the data were carefully recorded on chart paper that was posted around the room. As we reviewed the data at the conclusion of the meeting, a picture began to emerge of a faculty with many assets, including the willingness to work together to improve literacy instruction.

Shortly after this session, the team and I met to debrief on the experience and discuss the data. As we talked about how the meeting had gone, it was clear that the team, particularly the teachers, felt empowered by the success of the session. The teachers reported that they had received positive feedback from the faculty, and they were anxious to build on the momentum.

To make sense of the data, we posted the chart paper around the room and examined it. The data were arranged according to the questions that generated the data. The overarching question was, What does a balanced literacy classroom look like? Under this were three subquestions: (a) What is the teacher doing? (b) What are the students doing? and (c) What does the room look like? My role was to ask questions to help the team think about what they saw in the data and what meaning they made of it. As the team members studied the data, they began to identify categories into which the discrete pieces of data could be organized. As the data were rearranged, I asked the team to tell me what they saw. The team pointed out that the category of "resources needed," which was essentially a list of materials the teachers indicated they needed to create balanced literacy classrooms, was the largest category. The conversation then quickly turned to a discussion of developing an action plan to get the teachers what they needed so they could implement balanced literacy strategies. Carefully trying not to stifle the team's enthusiasm, but wanting to keep the team focused on analyzing the data, I asked the team whether we could set the resource data aside for now and look at the other data categories.

As the team studied the other categories, one of the teachers remarked that she saw contradictions in the data. She noted that some of the data related to what a teacher does in a balanced literacy classroom did not seem to fit with what the team had read in books and journal articles about balanced literacy or what the literacy specialist from Texas State had presented. Another teacher, who worked in a support role and therefore had an opportunity to visit many classrooms, indicated that she too saw contradictions. But the contradictions she saw were in what the teachers said students were doing in a balanced literacy classroom and what she typically saw students doing in the classrooms she visited. This led to a discussion about the limits of self-reported data and the importance of multiple data sources. In the end, the team concluded that more data were needed before they could determine what resources the teachers needed. However, there was one conclusion the team could draw from the data they had: Teachers had various levels of understanding about the components of balanced literacy. As a result, developing a common understanding became the team's focus.

The following week, the team met again, this time to develop an action plan. The team members, particularly Amy, the principal, had many ideas about how to proceed. Again, my role was one of asking questions. My aim was to prompt the group to think carefully through the proposal, particularly as it related to maintaining communication between the work of the leadership team and the faculty as a whole. Additionally, because I had engaged in a similar process as a principal, I was able to offer resources, such as suggested readings and strategies. By the end of the meeting, the team was well on its way to having a workable action plan. Over the next month, the team met on its own to complete the plan.

I did not know it at the time, but this was the beginning of the team becoming increasingly self-directed. Although I continued to meet with the team regularly over the course of the next year and I occasionally provided direct support, such as conducting training sessions for the faculty and giving assistance with data collection, the team took responsibility for implementing the plan. My primary role was to help the team think through problems that arose and to encourage them to continue when the work got hard. As the year progressed, the team began to fulfill even these roles for themselves and, although present, I became much less a part of the work.

Implementing the Plan

In developing the action plan, the leadership team considered the importance of providing multiple and varied opportunities for Caulfield teachers to learn about balanced literacy classrooms. The team used existing structures such as whole-school workshops and grade-level meetings as vehicles to deliver consistent content to the entire faculty. The team also created new structures, including book study teams and informal discussion groups, to allow for differentiated professional development based on teacher interest. The purposeful attention to providing consistent content and allowing for individual interest was key to the success of the plan.

Through a series of six professional development workshops, Caulfield teachers learned about various aspects of balanced literacy from external consultants. Grade-level meetings were then used as follow-up sessions in which teachers discussed what they learned in the workshops and how they were applying this learning to their practice. As part of the discussion, teachers often shared artifacts of their work, such as videos and student work samples. The teacher from each grade level who also served on the leadership team shared the artifacts with the leadership team so that the team could see how the work was progressing across the school.

By making balanced literacy the focus of grade-level meetings, the leadership team changed the nature of the meetings. Previously, grade-level meetings had been primarily managerial. In asking teachers to discuss their work, the leadership team transformed grade-level meetings into ongoing professional development sessions. In this way, the leadership team increased time for professional development without adding to the already busy schedules of teachers. Moreover, by using a meeting that teachers were already obligated to attend, the leadership team ensured that even reluctant teachers would remain part of the conversation.

For teachers who were interested in learning more or who wanted additional opportunities beyond grade-level meetings to discuss their work, the leadership team set up book study groups and held "literacy happy hours." To facilitate the book study, the leadership team identified a list of books related to balanced literacy. Some of the books were general overviews of balanced literacy, whereas others focused on specific topics such as guided reading or interactive writing. Using grant funds provided by the Network, the leadership team purchased several copies of each book. They then presented the books to the teachers and asked them to select a book of interest. Based on this input, book study groups were formed, each with a leadership team member to facilitate the process. Groups met at various times, including over the summer months. When a group concluded their book study they made a brief presentation to the faculty so that others could learn from their work. The presentations also served as a way to encourage those who had not yet joined a book study group. By the end of the second year, almost every teacher had participated in at least one book study.

Along with facilitating the book studies, leadership team members sponsored "literacy happy hours." These informal after-school meetings occurred monthly at local restaurants. The purpose of holding the meetings away from the school was to create a more relaxed atmosphere and to reduce the likelihood that the meeting would be interrupted by other school business. Each meeting focused on a particular instructional strategy, such as word walls or mini-lessons. At least one leadership team member attended each meeting and served as a facilitator. Additionally, the leadership team recruited teachers whom they perceived as having some knowledge of the particular strategy. The recruited teachers shared their experience and answered questions for other teachers who were interested but had not yet tried the strategy or were struggling with it. Because the leadership team was careful to choose a variety of teachers to serve as "strategy specialists," rather than allowing one or two people to become "the expert," an internal support network among the teachers was created.

Outcomes

As a result the multifaceted action plan, by the end of the second year there was a noticeable change at Caulfield. Basal and worksheet-driven lessons had largely been replaced by small-group instruction that allowed students to actively engage with a variety of texts. Student work samples provided evidence that students had a voice in what they were reading and writing. Moreover, evaluation survey data from students and teachers were encouraging. The student survey data indicated that students liked the changes in literacy instruction and that they were confident in their abilities as readers and writers. Similarly, the teacher survey data suggested that teachers were seeing positive impacts from the balanced literacy initiative and they wanted to learn more.

Because the aim of the School Improvement Network was to help schools develop internal systems to support action research as a tool for continuous school improvement, Network schools were limited to two years of direct support from a Network critical friend. As the Caulfield team met at the conclusion of the second year, we discussed what the change in support would mean for the team. There was some discussion about lobbying the Network coordinator to allow Caulfield to continue in the Network for another year. And while it was affirming to know the team valued my contributions, I recognized a danger in this discussion. One of the challenges critical friends face is preventing the relationship from becoming one of dependency. Unlike consultants, who often benefit when schools continue services, a critical friend seeks to create an environment in which his or her support is no longer necessary. In fact, developing a sense of efficacy on the part of the "befriended" is a characteristic that distinguishes a critical friend from other forms of external support (MacBeath, 1998). If the Caulfield team believed that I was a necessary for the work to continue, then I had not done my job as a critical friend.

To get a sense of how the team viewed their ability to move forward without Network support, I suggested we talk about the team's strengths and areas they wanted to continue to develop. As we reflected about the work we had done and how the process had unfolded, we agreed that, although we initially worked in fits and starts, we had managed to grow into a high-functioning team. We had systems for gathering and analyzing data, a schedule and structure for meetings, a process for developing action plans, and a method for ensuring the work continued in a recursive pattern between the eight-member school improvement team and the larger body of the faculty as a whole. Through this review, it became clear that the team was well prepared to continue the work even without the questioning and prodding of a critical friend. If any team members had doubts about this, a culminating Network event would illustrate that Caulfield was more than capable of moving forward on its own.

In May of the second year, NCSI sponsored a conference for local schools. In addition to a nationally known keynote speaker, the conference included presentations by the leadership teams from Network schools highlighting the progress of their collaborative action research projects. For their presentation, Caulfield created an electronic portfolio of their work. The portfolio included student work samples, classroom videos, and artifacts such as instructional tools and guidelines for creating balanced literacy classrooms. The portfolio illustrated significant change as a result of the two years of action research at Caulfield. As the Caulfield team concluded their presentation, many of those in attendance sought out the team to ask questions about how they had accomplished the work. Team members adeptly answered questions and offered suggestions for initiating the process at other schools. There was encouragement to deliver the presentation at a national reading conference.

Lessons Learned

The Caulfield experience represents a successful critical friendship. Although we unquestionably had challenges and I made mistakes, we were able to work through those to support the school's improvement efforts. What, then, can be learned from this case study that will inform those who assume the role of critical friend? For me, there are three important lessons I take from my work as a critical friend at Caulfield: (a) the need to gain entry by establishing credibility, (b) the need to negotiate multiple relationships, and (c) the need to both support and challenge the school conducting the action research.

Gaining entry. As an outsider coming into a school, a critical friend must be thoughtful about the process of gaining entry to the school. It is a mistake to assume that an entry has been made simply because a school has committed to having a critical friend. Gaining entry is more than being allowed to work with a school; it is being welcomed and supported in the work. As some Network critical friends discovered, gaining entry can be the most challenging aspect of the critical friendship.

A critical entry point is with the principal. Although some principals may welcome any form of external support, most principals are more cautious. Because they are held responsible for school performance, principals want to know that having a critical friend will benefit the school in a significant way. School leaders are inundated with external consultants who offer quick fixes for school improvement, which often turn out to be costly and ineffective and can wreak havoc on a school (Fullan, 2001b). Critical friends must understand that principals have good reason to be skeptical and should view the skepticism as an opportunity for discussion rather than a roadblock. The conversations Amy and I had following the initial Network schools meeting allowed her to ask questions and to gain some assurance that working with a critical friend was likely to help the school move forward. Just as importantly, those conversations helped Amy see me as a trusted colleague rather than a threat or a nuisance.

A second critical point of entry is with the faculty. As with principals, faculty may view the critical friend with skepticism. Having seen external consultants come and go, faculty want to know how a critical friendship will be different. In essence, they want to know whether the investment of their time with the critical friend will be worth it. Again, this requires that the critical friend spend time listening to and talking with faculty. In the case of my work with Caulfield, the discussion we had at the first meeting of the School Improvement Network played an important role in my gaining entry with the faculty. When I met with the faculty as a whole, it was the teachers on the leadership team who introduced me to their colleagues, an act that suggested I could be trusted. While this gave me an in with the faculty, I continually justified my entry in the school by regularly interacting with the faculty and by responding to individual e-mail inquiries from teachers.

Negotiating multiple relationships. Critical friendships often take the form of one-to-one relationships in which the critical friend works with an individual teacher or school leader. In the case of the Network schools, the critical friend served a team of educators. Serving as a critical friend to a team creates a responsibility for the critical friend to carefully negotiate the relationship to prevent the appearance that the interests of some team members are being prioritized over others. The effectiveness of the critical friendship can be diminished if the critical friend is seen to be allied with particular team members rather than the team as a whole (MacBeath, 1998). This is especially true when the team is comprised of both teachers and school leaders, two groups whose interests are often viewed as conflicting.

In working with the Caulfield team, I was constantly aware of the need to maintain a neutral stance. Because of my work as a principal and as a faculty member in an educational leadership program, I had a natural affiliation with the administrators on the team. At the same time, I knew that if the teachers saw me as aligned with administration, my credibility as a critical friend would suffer. As a result, I carefully monitored my interactions with the group, particularly in the early stages of the project, when we had yet to firmly establish our working relationship as a team. I selected my words purposefully. I asked questions to elicit perspectives from all team members. And I tried to avoid becoming the deciding factor in conflicts. In many ways, this was one of the most challenging aspects of being a critical friend. A number of times there was a clear difference of opinion among team members, typically with Amy and Jon and a teacher or two on one side and the remaining teachers on the other. Inevitably, someone in the group would ask me to weigh in on the discussion. Often, I agreed with one perspective over the other, yet I resisted coming out and saying this. First, to have done so would have been akin to my assuming the role of expert, which was not my aim. Secondly, if I agreed with Amy and Jon, I risked being seen as simply an extension of the school leadership and, therefore, not a critical friend that could be trusted by the teachers. Conversely, if I agreed with the teachers, I risked being viewed as undermining the leaders' credibility. Negotiating this tension between providing constructive critique and maintaining neutrality was quite difficult and required that I consciously assess whose critical friend I was perceived to be. But it was not always readily evident how various members of the school community perceived me. I found that periodically checking in with individual members of the team allowed me to gauge how I was being viewed and to correct any unintentional messages I had sent that suggested I favored one perspective over another.

Support and challenge. Serving in the role of critical friend means providing both support and challenge (Watling et al., 1998). The question is when and how much? In working with Caulfield, I assumed, as had been the case in my previous work as a critical friend, that in the early stages of the relationship my role would be primarily one of friend; that is a supportive role. Only after establishing a trusting relationship would I be the critic who challenges the team.

Because I was using this frame of reference, I was initially cautious in my approach with Caulfield. I made contact to let Amy know I was available to help, but not wanting to intrude or be a burden, especially to Amy as she settled into the principalship, I did not push when the team did not attend a meeting or did not appear to follow through with part of the plan. Because I did not believe we yet had a strong enough relationship to allow me to question or challenge, I essentially waited and hoped that the team would at some point be ready to turn their attention to the action research project.

As it turned out, this approach was not what Caulfield needed. My initial passive approach only served to allow the project to become less of a priority. Once I began to push the team to set goals and specific dates for accomplishing tasks, they responded by becoming more active and quickly moved the project forward.

In reflecting upon this, I came to see that the support and challenge roles of a critical friend are more intertwined than I had previously understood. Prior to my work with Caulfield, I viewed support and challenge almost as opposite forces on a lever with the critical friend intermittently applying support to reassure the befriended or pressure to prompt action. In this model, as one force is increased, the other is consequently decreased. After working with Caulfield, I had to rethink this notion because, for Caulfield, I often applied pressure and support simultaneously rather than intermittently. There were times when the team needed only support or pressure, but more often they needed both at the same time. They needed me to ask the difficult questions that would help them broaden their perspectives and understand the challenge before them. They also needed assurance that they were capable of addressing the issues we uncovered. In this way, support and challenge function like the strands of a rope. Twisted together they are stronger than either is individually.

CONCLUSION

The portfolio the Caulfield team presented at the Network conference clearly suggests the school benefited from its affiliation with the School Improvement Network. My own reflection about the experience just as clearly illustrates that I, too, gained from the relationship. Working in an educational leadership program, I spend a great deal of time reading and talking about schools. The schools I read about are abstract places I have spent little or no time in. What I know of the schools comes from reading a researcher's perspective or briefly visiting a student in his or her classroom. This limited perspective obscures my understanding of the complexity of school improvement. Being a critical friend gave me a connection to a real school with real issues. As part of the leadership team, I was immersed in the context of the school and shared responsibility for the work the school was doing. This connection helped me remember what a difficult and complex endeavor school improvement is, and the important role a critical friend can play in that process.

CHAPTER 3

Collaborative Action Research as a Laboratory for Graduate Education

Charles L. Slater

Charles Slater taught graduate classes at Texas State University that assisted School Improvement Network schools with their action research. Charles also was a critical friend to one of the Network schools.

THE MOVIE *ONCE* is a romantic comedy from Ireland about a poor young couple (Collins, Niland, & Carney, 2007). The boy plays the guitar on the street, and the girl persuades a shopkeeper to let her play one of the pianos for sale. Together, they make harmony. The ending is not Hollywood—they return to their first loves, but not before the boy buys her a piano, which she keeps on playing.

The movie could be a metaphor for the School Improvement Network. K–12 and the university came together temporarily to make music but ultimately we returned to our own sectors. The hope is that the relationship will help us both to continue to play music. This chapter will describe a variety of ways in which graduate students in education benefited from involvement in collaborative action research.

THEORETICAL CONSIDERATIONS IN COLLABORATIVE ACTION RESEARCH

Albert Einstein described gravity as a warping of space and time. It is like a bowling ball on a trampoline. When several billiard balls are rolled onto the trampoline, they appear to be attracted to the bowling ball, but of course it is the field that creates the attraction (Isaacson, 2007). Soon after Einstein, Kurt Lewin (1948) applied field theory to social science. He introduced action research, describing it as research for social management or social engineering that leads to action: "Research that produces nothing but books will not suffice" (pp. 202–203). In education, the idea is that teachers can be researchers. They define questions, gather data, and make changes.

Anderson and Herr (1999) suggested criteria for rigor in action research that are similar to the interactions Gordon described in his discussion of the integrative power of action research in the Introduction. *Outcome validity* in this type of research depends on the extent to which the problem is solved or reframed in a more complicated way. *Process validity* includes reflective cycles, examination of assumptions, ongoing learning, evidence for assertions, and multiple sources of evidence. *Democratic validity* addresses the degree of collaboration of stakeholders. *Catalytic validity* reorients and focuses the energy of participants. *Dialogic validity* refers to the need for peer review.

Anderson and Herr (1999) worried that this type of insider research would be co-opted by a nonreflective school culture. Done well, it requires extensive discussion at the problem definition stage. John Smyth (1989) described the necessary stages in his frequently quoted article on critical reflection. He wanted teachers to "uncover the forces that inhibit and constrain them" (p. 2). Smyth's four steps for doing this are "(a) describing (What do I do?), (b) informing (What does this mean?), (c) confronting (How did I come to be like this?), and (d) reconstructing (How might I do things differently?)" (p. 2).

Graduate students in the course Continuous School Improvement attempted to assist Network schools through Smyth's four steps. This assistance was intended not only to help school practitioners with action research but also to foster experiential, reflective learning for graduate students. In the next part of this chapter I will describe the types of assistance and learning activities that graduate students engaged in with Network schools. Later in the chapter I will extend the discussion of student involvement in action research to cross-cultural research carried out by graduate students in Mexico.

ASSISTANCE AND LEARNING IN NETWORK SCHOOLS

Graduate students assisted Network schools to initiate their action research by helping administrators and teachers describe their schools, select focus areas, review and summarize literature, gather and analyze data, and design action plans. Here I will provide some snapshots of student activities.

Format of the Graduate Class

Schools were at different points in the development of their projects. They ranged from a high school with a survey ready to be analyzed and specific questions for a literature review to a school that wanted help but was not sure what kind. The action research team at the latter school had just been reconstituted under a new principal, and team members were only beginning the action research process. The principals at those Network schools who wanted graduate student assistance came to my Continuous School Improvement class to describe their schools and their projects. These exploratory sessions led to informal contracts with teams of graduate students. The graduate students visited the school they were assigned to and communicated regularly with the principal and teachers. Meanwhile, I helped students design assistance plans to guide their work. Examples of topics Network schools sought assistance with included guided reading, bilingual education, school climate, alternative education models, ninth-grade retention, a high school reading survey analysis, and peer coaching. The culminating product of each graduate student team was a written report concerning the requested assistance to be presented to the Network school.

Getting Started

To provide them with practice observing and describing, I asked the graduate students (all either current or former practitioners) to describe their own schools. We then asked the Network schools that wished to work with us to describe *their* schools in order to provide a context for the action research. Both graduate students and practitioners from Network schools had a tendency to overestimate what others knew about their schools. One of my roles in this process was to ask probing questions to help participants amplify their descriptions. For example, I asked a leader from an alternative high school to write answers to the following questions:

- Why was the alternative school created?
- Can anyone attend?
- How long do students stay?
- What are the student demographics?
- What is their level of achievement?
- Can they work from home?

Another type of early assistance was helping Network schools to define their focus areas. One school decided they wanted to improve students' social skills. We helped the school specify the social skills to which they were referring and gather evidence showing that the current level of social skills was inadequate. We also worked with Network schools to develop problem statements that were clear and complete. Finally, we assisted Network schools to write measurable improvement objectives. The students and I observed considerable improvement from first to final drafts of school descriptions, focus areas, and improvement objectives.

Researching and Presenting Alternatives

Once schools have decided on their action research focus area and improvement objectives, they often can request assistance identifying and exploring alternative improvement programs or activities prior to designing their action plan. Graduate students can research alternatives by completing and summarizing literature reviews and by identifying promising practices in other schools. They have experience working on literature reviews as part of their graduate program, and as graduate students they need to become familiar with the library and assorted databases. Students can also identify promising practices through Internet searches, school visits, and conversations with practitioners.

Two action research projects illustrate the help that graduate students can offer. One focused on fourth-grade writing and the other on elementary mathematics.

One elementary school was most appreciative of receiving help on its fourth-grade writing project. When looking at the fourth-grade writing test scores for the previous school year, the school decided there was room for improvement. Graduate students identified three related topics in the literature: the focus of lessons, the importance of rigor, and approaches to best practices. They presented three alternative programs: The New Jersey Writing Project could help focus lessons, a self-regulated reading initiative could raise the level of rigor in classrooms, and backward design was an example of a best practice.

The students described the first alternative, the New Jersey Writing Project. The philosophy emphasizes process, idea generation, and multiple drafts. Implementation begins with three-week intensive, research-based inservice training for teachers that draws connections between all subjects and writing. It gives teachers tools to successfully implement a writer's workshop and helps make writing the focus of school lessons. The second alternative was designated daily reading and writing times to help teachers increase rigor and to promote self-regulated reading and writing. The graduate students reported research that concluded students in self-regulated classrooms had higher achievement as well as more positive attitudes.

The students also reported that classroom libraries with appropriate grade-level texts can engage students at varying reading levels. The third alternative was backward design, a teaching process by which students help to create rubrics before they start an assignment. Rubrics include descriptors of the learning. They start with the end and work backward to the learning activities. The graduate students recommended readings on each alternative and suggested that teachers be provided opportunities to explore and fully understand their action plan.

Another elementary school was most concerned about mathematics achievement. The school motto is "What I will be is up to me!!" The school's vision statement is

> We will create a supportive, secure and dynamic environment where everyone, through a team effort, participates in the growth and development of the whole child. Children are expected to meet high academic standards. With excitement for learning, our students will grow into successful, life-long learners.

The school's focus area was to develop a new math curriculum to expand student knowledge in math, increase math scores, and ultimately become an exemplary school.

The school's principal visited the university class and asked graduate students to investigate Mountain Math, Mrs. Fritzie, gifted and talented enrichment, vertical alignment, journal daily math, common vocabulary, and content in the state curriculum which was not addressed in the school's curriculum. The graduate students developed a report for the school addressing each topic.

Unplanned Change

Action research is not only intended to address school-based problems. It can also have implications for theory. Schoenfeld (1999) outlined issues of practice that might contribute to theory. He called them sites of progress: curriculum development that gets at what it means to know and be able to do something, assessment that relates the measure to the desired outcome, the careful study of unplanned change as it occurs in schools, and examination of the professional lives of teachers.

One elementary school my students and I worked with was a good example of unplanned change. The school had just opened with 550 students. It is one of two schools to serve as a bilingual cluster in the school district. The majority of the students were bused from different communities around the district. The campus was 72% Hispanic, 15% African American, 5% White, and 3% Asian. The school's leadership team selected the following goal:

> *To improve reading comprehension so that students will be proficient readers. We want our students' reading performance to meet the district's standards. We want to close the gap in reading performance between our monolingual and bilingual students by ensuring that our teachers have the knowledge, skill, and commitment to effectively implement reading improvement strategies.*

Two of my graduate students worked with the school in the fall to compile a list of resources for nonfiction comprehension strategies, identify publishers of bilingual texts, and find experts in reading comprehension strategies who could conduct staff development sessions. In the spring, a graduate student worked with the school to assist in mathematics. That student helped to organize a "Math Family Night." Later that spring, other graduate students designed a questionnaire to help the school identify its level of implementation of guided reading.

The principal and the leadership team were excited to be opening a new school and optimistic about success for their students. They were proud to be one of the two bilingual cluster schools in the district. However, after a few months, the principal left to take a new position, and the leadership team found it difficult to communicate with the rest of the faculty. Some were strongly in favor of the guided reading approach; others were reticent. The divide seemed to fall between bilingual and regular education teachers.

The team faithfully attended Network workshops and participated enthusiastically. However, there was little communication between the school and the university between workshops, except for the school's work with the graduate classes and my visits as the school's critical friend. In the summer before what would have been the school's second year in the School Improvement Network, the new principal decided that the school would drop out of the Network.

This experience raises several questions about the philosophical differences between bilingual and regular education teachers. Did the greater interest of one group hinder the involvement of the other? Is stable principal leadership one of the necessary conditions to overcome differences between faculty groups? How did racial and cultural issues between the two groups affect the interaction? Questions like these can be addressed by graduate students in post-analyses of action research efforts.

Lessons in Leadership

One advantage of the graduate students' work with schools engaged in action research was the opportunity to interact with school principals, both in the university classroom and at the schools. Most of the principals the students worked with were dynamic leaders committed to developing their schools as centers of inquiry and their teachers as reflective inquirers. A few of the principals were struggling with their leadership role, but interaction with these principals also led to student learning.

One principal appeared to endorse teacher involvement in action research and expressed readiness to cooperate with data collection, workshops, and anything that could lead to school improvement. However, the principal's stated openness seemed to belie the reticence of the staff to participate in action research. Graduate students puzzled over this difference between the stated desires of the principal and survey results, which indicated little progress in the focus area. Another principal did not seem to grasp issues related to the school's focus area and expressed an offhand attitude about how to plan for improvement. The graduate students wondered how this principal could be an effective leader. During a confidential class discussion, the students discussed qualities of good and poor leadership. A third principal identified student behavior as a problem for action research. This administrator brought extensive teacher survey data to the graduate class, but none of the data indicated a problem with student discipline. Although the principal expressed concern about the manners and politeness of students, there was little evidence that teachers or assistant principals shared this concern. The principal had not involved them in identifying the school's focus area. Graduate students asked why the administrator had defined student behavior as the main problem. What were teachers most concerned about? They wondered if the principal had simply substituted her own opinion in place of a more careful look at issues in the school.

Assessing Whole-School Improvement

Accountability systems have encouraged much discussion about using test results to improve instruction (Johnson, 2002). The popular term is *data-driven,* and the intent is to use tests to drive academic achievement for all groups of students. Unfortunately, the term implies frenetic action accompanied by simplistic thinking.

Scores up,
Scores down,
Make a change, and
See what comes 'round.

The terms *data-informed* or *data-reflective* are more consistent with the spirit of action research. It is better to make time to involve stakeholders democratically and analyze problems in way that encourages different points of view.

One Network middle school was developing a comprehensive improvement plan and needed help to develop and analyze a teacher survey. In her second year, the principal had started the school year with goals that were collaboratively developed with faculty. Three of the school's goals were to (a) develop a campus vision based on supporting student achievement for all students; (b) create collaborative time for teachers to reflect, discuss, and analyze instruction; and (c) find other professional development opportunities for teachers based on individual, team, or content area needs. As a result of the year's professional development and collaboration, the campus developed not only a vision but also a "Pyramid of Interventions," a system of multiple levels of support systems and strategies for intervening to help struggling students.

Student achievement at the school had increased during the first year of action research, and the leadership team wanted to understand what teachers believed had the largest impact as well as what needed to be the focus for the upcoming school year in order to continue the improvement of teaching. Graduate students were asked to assist with two surveys designed to identify patterns of effectiveness and areas for improvement in professional development. A professional development survey was completed by 100% of the teachers, and a student achievement analysis survey was completed by subject area teams. The graduate students concluded that (a) analyzing data to improve instruction and (b) collaboration time with fellow teachers were the most highly rated activities. Sixty-eight percent of the teachers surveyed said classroom-based assistance was the most effective type of professional development for them. Ninety-seven percent of teachers felt collaboration time supported the vision of the school. Collaboration was said to have the most positive impact on student achievement, followed in order by focused workshops, peer coaching, peer facilitation, and lastly, conferences that cover multiple topics.

These middle school surveys are a good example of graduate students working with a school to assist with whole-school improvement. The survey analysis helped the school to measure progress and to move the action research forward.

ACTION RESEARCH IN MEXICO

The examples of action research reported thus far came from Texas. Action research is also an international endeavor, as Kurt Lewin envisioned:

> No one working in the field of inter-group relations can be blind to the fact that we live today in one world. . . . Inter-group relations in this country will be formed to a large degree by the events on the international scene and particularly by the fate of colonial peoples. . . . It will be crucial whether or not the policy of this country will follow a policy of the colonial empires. Or will we follow . . . a pattern which leads gradually to independence, equality and co-operation? . . . A large scale effort of social research on inter-group relations doubtless would be able to have a lasting effect on the history of this country. . . . It needs courage as Plato defines: "Wisdom concerning dangers." (Lewin, 1948, pp. 215–216)

The future of action research could lie in cross-cultural groups working in local contexts. A first step in this direction is for students to gain perspective by exploring work going on in other countries and examining issues that matter to the development of education in a democracy. Here I will examine an example of action research in graduate education in Mexico.

Graduate students in a doctoral program in Mexico followed an action research process similar to those in Texas. However, they did not have the benefit of a network of schools undertaking action research projects, nor were there prearranged contacts with school principals. Nonetheless, the graduate students were able to work in teams to identify projects in schools and colleges where they worked.

In one Mexican class, graduate students who also taught at La Universidad de la Sierra (The University of the Sierras) studied the clash of cultures between undergraduate students from rural areas and the demands of a new university. Young men expressed preferences to go north to the United States rather than develop higher education skills that might not lead to a job in Mexico. Young women were reluctant to come to school and preferred to stay in the rural areas where they grew up.

La Universidad de la Sierra is located in Moctezuma in the state of Sonora, Mexico. This is a rural location that serves 30 municipalities. It was founded on April 12, 2002, in response to demands by the people in the region to have an institution of higher education in the mountains of Sonora. The area had fallen behind in the last few decades and population had decreased. Many emigrated to the United States. Young people who stayed in the area preferred to work on ranches rather than seek more education. The challenge for higher education was how to attract these young people and induce them to remain in Mexico rather than emigrate. Young people were needed to maintain and grow the economy, culture, and education of the region.

The graduate students pointed out the great disparity between urban and rural areas of Mexico. Indigenous groups live isolated from the rest of the economy of the country. For Mexico to develop, it would need to address the disparities between social groups: those in extreme poverty and the elites. To keep pace with other countries, Mexico would also need to invest in education. Per-pupil expenditure at the primary level in 2004 was under $2,000 (U.S.), whereas the United States spent over $8,000 per pupil (Organization for Economic Cooperation and Development, 2007).

The graduate students explored the reasons why marginalized zones had limited education. Parents had few resources. They could not pay tuition. Students had limited educational preparation. Indigenous communities were often isolated from the economy of the rest of the country.

One way that Mexico has been addressing these needs is to expand higher education opportunities. Across Mexico, the number of institutions of higher education has increased dramatically: from 118 in 1970 to more than 1,292 in 1998. The number of students in these institutions increased from 250,000 to 1,727,500 in the same period. The Constitution of 1917 established two fundamental principles: First, there should be balance between economic and social development, and second, economic development should be an instrument for social justice, distributing goods and services throughout the country.

The graduate students studied the motives of young people as they decided whether to continue their education. They looked at the number of graduates from feeder schools that sent students to the university. The number had gone steadily down from 64% in 2002 to 24% in 2005.

Next, they interviewed 20 of the students to identify issues of concern. One problem was that the university did not offer a wide range of careers. There was a lack of congruence between the curricula in the feeder schools and in the university. There was an apparent contradiction between the structural needs of the university and the interests and orientations of the students. There were scholarships from the federal government. The Programa Nacional de Becas a la Educación Superior (Nacional Program of Educational Scholarships) provided aid to 50% of students from La Universidad de la Sierra.

The graduate students developed alternative solutions. The first was for the university to integrate the social and academic needs of the students. The students suggested that the university offer practical options that would appeal to and garner support from various government programs. From a cultural point of view, the family is linked directly with the development of natural resources: ranching, agriculture, mining, crafts, and tourism. Masculine and feminine roles are determined and differentiated from an early age, and young men participate in supporting the family. Three competing images occupy the young person: continue to work with the family, study to improve the economic condition, or emigrate to the United States.

The second solution was to design interinstitutional programs. The university majors are not directly related to the previous studies of the students. The feeder school programs could be redesigned for a better fit. The third solution was to make connections between the universities and diverse sectors of the economy. There could also be better connections with business and industry in the area. The fourth solution was to make better sociocultural connections with the surrounding community. Finally, the graduate students suggested strategies to improve communication among institutions of higher education.

CONCLUSION

Graduate student evaluations of the classes in Texas and Mexico were generally positive. They liked working on real projects that would benefit a school and students rather than on purely academic exercises. Some cited the disadvantages of not having a clearly defined project at the beginning of the course and experiencing confusion as they struggled through the project. Such is the trade-off of learning in action: The gain is relevance, and the loss is simplicity. Participating in action research is messier than a syllabus with weekly lectures, assigned readings, and a paper due at the end of the semester.

Educational leadership programs can contribute to graduate students', schools', and universities' understanding of action research by making participation in action research part of the graduate curriculum. The best approach is not only to tell graduate students about action research but also to involve them in doing action research. Action research, in my opinion, also is appropriate as the basis of master's theses and doctoral dissertations. Action research as master's or dissertation research matters not just to the graduate student but to the practitioners who both participate in the research and become a natural audience for the research report. Action research theses and dissertations can benefit real schools in the real world—not just sit on library shelves.

In the movie *Once* we are left wondering whether the boy and girl benefited from their temporary relationship. That is our question as well. Do graduate students benefit from participating in action research? The indications are that participating in action research has great potential to prepare graduate students to become better school leaders, reframe problems in a more complicated way, examine assumptions, collaborate democratically, focus team energy, and engage in reflective dialogue.

CHAPTER 4

Critical Engagement for Collaborative Action Research

John Smyth

John Smyth was a visiting scholar at Texas State University while the School Improvement Network was in operation. He provided informal consultation to the Network.

The academy must become a more vigorous partner in the search for answers to our most pressing social, civic, economic and moral problems, and must affirm its historic commitment to what I call the scholarship of engagement. (Boyer, 1996, p. 13)

LATER IN THE PAPER from which this quote came, the late Ernest Boyer (1996) captured in a handful of carefully chosen words the whole reason why universities might want to increasingly (and as a matter of some urgency) participate in collaborative action research:

Increasingly, the campus is being viewed as a place where students get credentialed and faculty get tenured, while the overall work of the academy does not seem particularly relevant to the nation's most pressing . . . problems. (p. 15)

There it is in a nutshell! Boyer's challenge is just as urgent now, if not more so, than it was when he uttered it over a decade ago. The question is whether we have the moral courage and fiber to go down the pathway described with such clarity by Boyer, especially in a political climate that is increasingly hostile to such avowedly political work by universities.

In this chapter I will examine five key propositions, and their associated arguments and questions, which are central to the advancement and involvement of universities in collaborative action research. These propositions focus on the following topics:

- Commitment to social justice
- Authentic and inclusive collaboration
- Ethical and methodologically respectful practices
- Construction of an emancipatory knowledge base
- Vigorous pursuit of academic freedom

In the process of pursuing these propositions I will connect my ideas and arguments with the Principles and Goals of the National Center for School Improvement's (NCSI) School Improvement Network. To achieve this I will shorthand them throughout the chapter as Principle 1, Goal 1, and so forth, as they appear in Figure I.2 (page 11) of the opening chapter by Steve Gordon. And at the outset I wish to point out that whether or not individual Network schools were successful in their action research seemed to be related in no small measure to whether the schools (especially their principals) were able to align their action research projects to the Network's Principles and Goals.

The central theoretical idea explored in this chapter builds upon and extends what Fear, Rosaen, Bawden, and Foster-Fishman (2006) referred to as the process of "coming to critical engagement." At one level, this has to do with what Bond and Paterson (2005) referred to in their cryptic question "coming down from the ivory tower?" What they were alluding to was the manner and extent to which universities develop and pursue "civic and economic engagement with community"—that is to say, the agenda universities pursue around the interconnections between multiple missions of teaching, research, and service to the wider community (Network Principle 4). This is by no means an especially new or novel idea, as I will reveal shortly. On another level, what an examination of the critical engagement process injects into the discussion is the reality that when research has consequences for the community, the effect is that there is no such thing as remaining neutral, benign, objective, or value-free. There are always interests being served and others being denied, silenced, or marginalized in any research activity, and part of the research process *ought to* involve having the courage and commitment to making such interests public. In its most productive form, coming to critical engagement through collaborative action research means unmasking and unveiling how power structures work in and through constructed hierarchies of one kind and or another, and how such hierarchies operate to sustain and maintain privilege. Collaborative action research is a prime example of how critical engagement can be pursued between a university and a community (in this case, schools) in ways that produce forms of enhanced capacity-building in and between both (Network Goal 3).

The reason I commence this chapter on collaborative action research in universities by invoking Boyer is because he is probably the most coherent and eloquent exponent in recent times, anywhere in the world, on what can be gained from the mutual engagement of universities with the communities and societies in which they are embedded. To my mind, Boyer has been a crucial and seminal contributor to these arguments and debates, and we would do well to revisit and seriously heed his sage advice (Network Goal 1). One of the reasons Boyer was able to be so perceptive was because of his movement between the academy and government. He demonstrated a rare capacity to be extremely candid, as for example when he described what went on inside Washington as being "startlingly detached" (Boyer, 1996, p. 14) and as constituting an "impoverished cultural discourse" (p. 15). Reflecting on the rarefied atmospherics in the U.S. government, he said he could "recall literally hundreds of hours when we talked about the procedural aspects of our work and the legal implications, but I do not recall one occasion when someone asked, 'Should we be doing this in the first place?'" (p. 15). This is a profoundly moral question, and one rarely asked up front by governments, or by universities, for that matter (Network Principle 2).

What is especially distressing in these contemporary times of complex and protracted problems that require multiple perspectives, or what the British call "joined up" approaches, is that there is so little political will and imagination to actually do this. Boyer (1996) says this obdurate situation persists despite "Abundant evidence show[ing] that both civic and academic health of any culture is vitally enriched as scholars and practitioners speak and listen carefully to each other" (p. 15) (Network Principle 3). The classic exemplar according to Boyer is the 19th-century Swiss city of Basel, which was a vibrant place in which "civic and university life were inseparable. . . . The university was engaged in civic advancement, and the city was engaged in intellectual advancement, and the two were joined" (p. 15).

Boyer's landmark work when he was president of the Carnegie Foundation for the Advancement of Teaching and Learning came in the form of a clarion call for a "new paradigm of scholarship" (Boyer, 1990). The essence of his argument was that the work of the professoriate needed to be recast within four interlocking functions, listed here in short form:

1. *Scholarship of Discovery:* Are we doing cutting edge inquiry that is opening up new ideas?
2. *Scholarship of Integration:* Are we placing knowledge into larger patterns, constellations and contexts that can be understood by the wider community?
3. *Scholarship of Application:* How is this knowledge relevant and useful?
4. *Scholarship of Teaching and Learning:* How is our knowledge being made communal, and can others make sense of it?

Several years later Boyer (1996) went on to articulate an umbrella term for these four forms of scholarship, which he referred to as the work of an "engaged scholar" (p. 17), or "the scholarship of engagement." Driving him on this occasion was the deepening despair with which he witnessed the growing isolation and disconnectedness of universities from civic life (Network Goal 2). In his view, "our great universities simply cannot afford to remain islands of affluence, self-importance, and horticultural beauty in a sea of squalor, violence and despair" (p. 19).

Boyer's (1996) conviction as to what was required was a *scholarship of engagement* at two levels. At one level there was a need for "connecting the rich resources of the university to our most pressing social, civic and ethical problems . . ." (p. 19). Further, there was a second, deeper purpose or mission, in which "a special climate [is created] in which academic and civic cultures communicate more continuously and creatively with one another . . . to enlarge . . . the universe of human discourse and enrich . . . the quality of life of us all" (p. 20).

COMING TO CRITICAL ENGAGEMENT IN COLLABORATIVE ACTION RESEARCH

Drawing upon and extending Boyer's ideas, a group of scholars (Fear et al., 2006) from an agricultural extension background have recently begun to popularize the idea of critical engagement—which provides us with a useful theoretical turn within which to examine what occurs when universities embark on collaborative action research. These scholars draw their theoretical inspiration in part from Daniel Yankelovich's (1991) book *Coming to Public Judgment: Making Democracy Work in a Complex Society.* Critical engagement is code for exploring how the tectonic plates of capitalism are impacting differentially upon society and how some excluded groups might move beyond their current diminished capacity and assertively begin to push back. Part of what Yankelovich is concerned with is not only a critique of our seemingly unfettered infatuation with technical and expert values over more communal values, but also a critique of how this is occurring, along with an exploration of what a democratic alternative that works to change this situation might look like. Collaborative action research is one such possibility (Network Principle 2).

As far as I can discern, there are three key aspects in the process of coming to critical engagement that have important messages for processes like collaborative action research between university researchers and school practitioners, namely: (a) a journey of collaborative learning (Network Principle 1); (b) a notion of the "critical" that examines the concept of power, how things came to be the way they are, and how to improve the situation for the most excluded (Network Goal 5); and (c) "engagement" that asks questions about the moral imperative to engage in collegial interaction with communities in ways that emphasize visceral qualities such as self-determination, an ethic of co-ownership of processes and outcomes, open participation, distributive and decentralized leadership (Network Goal 3), and ways of working that minimize the extent of external management. Construed in this way, engagement is about the lived experiences of those pushed to the margins through no fault of their own, the conditions of their marginalization, and working to create the spaces from within which changes might occur.

Keeping in mind these three key aspects of critical engagement, let us dip in a little more detail into some topics that might cast light on not only *how* universities might engage in collaborative action research with schools, but more importantly *why.*

Commitment to Social Justice

As we saw in the Introduction, where Gordon systematically discussed the features of collaborative action research, there are a number of indispensable defining hallmarks that fit broadly within the following:

- A disciplined form of inquiry made public
- Small groups or communities of insiders and outsiders
- Gathering data for the provision of feedback
- Commitment to changing power relations
- Reflection and critique with the intent of adopting planned action
- Transforming school cultures and improving learning

- Local and immediate change as well as larger social change
- Commitment to ideas of democratic intent

In a paper entitled "Toward a Professional Community for Social Justice," Calderwood (2003) presented a list of reasons why teachers find it so difficult in the context of the normal course of their work to bring about small-scale change as well as wider social change, and why a commitment to social justice is such a difficult ideal to embark upon and to sustain for teachers (Network Principle 2). As Calderwood put it, for many teachers

> teaching for social justice is extremely challenging and sometimes professionally damaging. They find that their work is more solitary than communal. They see too little interprofession collegiality and shared purpose, due to heavy workloads and groaning resources. Burdened by numerous mandates, they often cannot lift their eyes, attention, or energy beyond their daily endeavors with students. (p. 301)

Notwithstanding the considerable definitional problems accompanying a term like *social justice*, which is open to debate and argument, is difficult to measure, and cannot be "shorn" of its semantic ambiguities and uncertainties, Frey, Pearce, Pollock, Artz, and Murphy (1996) provide a useful provisional starting point when they refer to social justice as an approach that involves "the engagement with and advocacy for those in our society who are economically, socially, politically, and/or culturally under-resourced" (p. 110) (Network Goal 5). Given that there can be no blueprint for social justice, the best we can hope for is to work toward "developing a sensibility for social justice" (p. 110). As Frey et al. note, this means a preparedness to hold back from trying to stipulate what a socially just society might look like, refraining from mandating a particular set of institutional arrangements, and generally acting in ways that convey the message that utopia is not just around the corner. At best, they say, we can only hope to work toward action within a framework of social justice sensibility that "(1) foregrounds ethical concerns; (2) commits to structural analyses of ethical problems; (3) adopts an activist orientation; (4) seeks identification with others" (p. 111).

Each of these points holds important implications for universities that embark on collaborative action research with schools for reasons of school improvement and enhanced learning. Yet, even before considering the first of these sensibilities, university researchers need to be animated to ask the most important socially critical question of all:

Whose interests are being served by our research? (Network Goal 1). There are several ways of addressing this question, but they all come back in essence to interrupting or puncturing the otherwise hierarchical and unmediated way in which power operates between university researchers and school people. At its most proximal level, and left to take its natural course, research will generally follow an exploitative line—that is to say, the researchers have the power, and school folk are compliant submissives, and research is done by the university types to school people, largely for the benefit of the academy (Network Principle 4). Although this description parodies the situation somewhat, the essence of it is roughly correct on many occasions.

How, then, can ethical concerns pervade research? There are several levels at which power can be mediated in order to transform the situation outlined above, including how and who frames research questions, whose language is allowed to prevail, who gets to be involved in the inquiry and in what fashion, how the process of sense-making occurs around the data, who participates in the sense-making, and in the end who owns the information collected and determines how it is to be used (Network Principle 3). These are all questions that, at one level, seem to be about procedure, but in reality, at a more profound level, they have to do with who has agency—meaningful power—over the destiny of the subjects of the research. Thus, operating ethically goes considerably beyond obtaining institutional review board or ethics committee approval, which is a thin view of ethics, to a much thicker view that is about interrupting the habitual power relationships around who does research, how, and for whom.

At a deeper level, university researchers undertaking research in schools also ought to be helping school people to ask questions such as

- How is what is going on here (in this school, classroom, curriculum, pedagogical practice) helping to improve the life chances of the *least advantaged* children or young people? (Network Principle 2)

Questions of this kind about the socially just nature of educational practices enable researchers and school practitioners to uncover and attend to the ways in which inequalities are knowingly or unwittingly reproduced in schools.

What does it mean to analyze ethical issues structurally? Many of the ordinary or mundane events that transpire in schools and classrooms are ascribed to

familiar patterns of origin or "causation," or are looked upon as a consequence of group or category membership attributed to students. For example,
when we say students are not learning (or are not achieving, or are failing),
what we are really saying is that (a) teachers are not teaching appropriately
or (b) students lack motivation, are not making sufficient effort, or come
from backgrounds that predispose them to being "at risk" (with considerations such as family, racial origin, ethnicity, class, or gender). Rarely do we
go to the level of seeking to ascertain whether there might be more distant
impediments or interferences that have to do with the way in which schooling itself is organized (largely in middle-class ways, as a matter of fact), using
forms of discourse and cultural patterns that are (however subtly or not)
unwelcoming and inhospitable to students from nondominant backgrounds
(Network Goal 4). In other words, at the most fundamental level there may
be a mismatch between the cultural attributes of the school and what it recognizes, and the cultural capital certain students bring with them to the
school. There may be an undisclosed agenda within the social fabric that is
largely invisible yet that produces injustice. Confronting structural impediments within an ethical sensibility in research means making the invisible
visible or, to put it another way, making the ordinary extraordinary.

Why is an activist orientation ethically important? The tenor of the discussion
thus far has suggested that when an interruption of power exposes social
structures (schools included) that support an unjust status quo, then it is
unethical to fail to upset or usurp the structure, or to allow the situation to
endure. In other words, research that unveils or unmasks the workings of
privilege and power is not neutral, objectivist, or value-free—it has an
agenda (as indeed does *all* research), which is to pursue a more democratic
intent, and in order to do that the existing state of affairs must be replaced
(Network Goal 2). Research with a socially just sensibility has a moral commitment to not merely uncover injustices or "bemoan the fact that some
people lack the minimal necessities of life. . . . [Instead, such research has]
a moral imperative to act as effectively as [it] can to do something about the
structurally sustained inequalities" (Frey et al., 1996, p. 111). This means
that collaborative action research is political in the sense that it is committed
to change (Network Principle 1), and it is advocacy-oriented in that it seeks
to work with or for the most marginalized and excluded. As Lather (1986)
put it, research of this kind is unashamedly, openly ideological.

What does seeking identification with others do? When we seek to identify or
develop solidarity with others through collaborative action research, what

is happening in terms of ethical sensibility is that we are embracing the concept that "none of us is truly free when some of us are oppressed" (Frey et al., 1996, p. 112). Those of us involved in collaborative action research need to see our work as being more than the sum of our individual research projects and instead as constituting part of a much wider set of narratives, which Race (2006) recently described most aptly as "using educational research when conceptually developing the good society" (p. 133) (Network Goal 2). The task is truly of that global order of magnitude, and we need to find the means to connect our stories with the narratives of others and in the process to better understand both them and ourselves.

Authentic and Inclusive Collaboration

The basic question to be asked here is whether the collaborative aspect of action research is "fake" or "real." What constitutes authenticity is a difficult philosophical question to answer, particularly when working across boundaries as significant as those presented between universities and schools. Although the literature on this topic is extensive and too detailed to canvass here, there are some key features that can be alluded to. In the end, recognizing authenticity is probably a matter of knowing it when you experience it!

The most important aspect of authentic collaboration, as already mentioned in this chapter, has to do with power, and in this case the question is not that different from the *in whose interests* question raised earlier. Put another way, what needs to be answered is

- Why are we in this?
- Who benefits?
- How can I feasibly involve others in collaboration? (Network Principle 4)

At the center here are significant issues of inequality. As John-Steiner, Weber, and Minnis (1998) say, "in most school-based research initiated by academics, researchers gain disproportionately in comparison with participating teachers from the work itself and related publications" (p. 774) (Network Goal 3). Herein lies the major challenge: "how to honor the voices of all participants [in ways in which] the entire project is jointly owned and produced and presented by teachers and researchers alike" (p. 774). Kreisberg (1992) summarized this as involving "developing questions, choosing methodology, and writing the results" (p. 230). What is at issue are several "value tensions" around "desires to learn and change [and] fears of self-exposure," as well as "status differences" based on prestige of respective institutions and what people hope or expect out of the collaboration (John-Steiner et al., 1998, p. 774).

Minnis, John-Steiner, and Weber (1994) provided a useful starting point when they defined collaboration in this context as involving a commitment to "not only plan, decide, and act jointly [but also] *think together,* combining independent conceptual schemes to create original frameworks" (cited in John-Steiner et al., 1998, p. 776) (Network Principle 2). At a practical level, this means having and continually demonstrating respect for the talents, resources, aspirations, and professional histories of each other:

> there is a commitment to shared resources, power and talent: no individual's point of view dominates, authority for decisions and actions resides in the group, and the work products reflect a blending of all participants' contributions. (p. 776)

The kinds of questions that often prove to be the most contentious in collaborative action research are around issues of:

- Differential time demands
- Competing obligations, loyalties, and expectations
- Differences in working methods
- Difficulties of writing together (p. 777)

An innovative way of tackling these issues, according to Clark et al. (1996), is to envisage the collaboration as "dialogue," and the way they approached it was through engaging in a Readers Theatre in which members of the group of researchers and teachers took turns at reading from the script of a play they had constructed from the transcripts of their collaborative research. Confronting the tensions in the collaboration in this way enabled them to keep a focus around matters such as

- Seeing their collaboration as evolving rather than fixed or dynamic
- Being open about the different reasons each had for being involved in the research
- Acknowledging one another's "positionality" (Lather, 1991), that is, what each brought to the collaboration
- Regarding teachers' improving teaching and learning as being crucial
- Developing a shared understanding of the common experience (Network Principle 2)

Although there are no formulas, silver bullets, or scripts to follow to ensure that collaboration will be authentic or inclusive, having some questions such as those listed above with which, on occasion, to arrest or interrogate the relationship is probably about as good as it is likely to get. That— and a modicum of goodwill and preparedness to include the wishes, perspectives, aspirations, and desires of the other party—will certainly go some way toward attaining the ideal of authenticity and inclusion in collaborative action research.

Ethical and Methodologically Respectful Practices

Linda Tuhiwai Smith (2005), speaking about indigenous research and methods that are committed to decolonizing approaches, describes the space between "research methodologies, ethical principles, institutional regulations, and human subjects and socially organized actors and communities" as being especially "tricky ground" (p. 85). By this she means that there are nuances in research relationships that must be continually negotiated and renegotiated, and this is something that must be done from a vantage point of give and take around "respect" (Network Goal 1). She asks the question, "what is respect, and how do we know when researchers are behaving respectfully?" (p. 97). Her response takes the form of what she terms a "bottom-up or community-up" (p. 97) approach to research conduct, some of the key features of which I can best summarize as

- Working in face-to-face ways rather than through distant forms of communication
- Looking and listening carefully before speaking
- Acknowledging that the researcher is "a learner"
- Not operating in paternalistic or patronizing ways
- Not flaunting knowledge in ways that amount to "showing off"
- Being "politically astute" in the sense of being attuned to avoiding pitfalls
- Finding ways of continually sharing knowledge (Network Goal 1)

Being ethical and respectful in collaborative action research, therefore, means holding and enacting a set of views that realistically deal with what Dorothy Smith (2005) calls "asymmetries of power" (p. 136). University researchers have power by virtue of their institutional status. Confronting these inequalities requires working with school practitioners in ways that acknowledge that

- They have worthwhile knowledge
- They may have different ways of framing questions
- They have language forms that differ from that of the academy
- They have worldviews that are equally valid

Kemmis and McTaggart (2005), both major international contributors to theorizing on the nature of collaborative or participatory action research, argue that "participatory action research opens communicative space between participants" (p. 576) through which mutual inquiry, intersubjective agreement, and joint action are possible (Network Principle 4). In addition to the well-recognized spiral of *plan, act and observe, reflect,* then *re-plan,* and so forth, Kemmis and McTaggart add that there are a number of key features all of which in some way address ethical and methodological respectfulness, most notably in terms of being

- *A social process:* in exploring the territory between the individual and the social
- *Participatory:* in that action research can only ever be "done on" ourselves and not "done to" others
- *Practical:* in the sense of seeking to improve the quality of the interactions people have and the way the interactions enhance their lives
- *Emancipatory:* in attempting to enable people to be released from unjust social structures (Network Principle 4)
- *Critical:* in seeking to facilitate ways in which people can recover alternative means of seeing, describing, and interacting with the world
- *Reflexive:* meaning "investigat[ing] reality in order to change it" and "chang[ing] reality in order to investigate it" (p. 567)
- *Transformative:* aiming to change theory in light of practice, and to better inform practice through theory (summarized on pp. 566–567)

Based on what has been discussed so far in this section, the kinds of questions that need, therefore, to be continuously foregrounded in ethical and methodological terms are

- Have we gone beyond a mechanical, instrumental, or institutional view of ethics?
- How do we know that?

- Have we developed a listening stance in the way we work?
- What is the evidence that our relationships are more horizontal than vertical?
- How are we "giving back" to our collaborators?
- Does our view of ethics go to the core of our action research relationships and the people we are working with?

In summary, it is my contention that when we feature these kinds of questions as a prominent component of collaborative action research, then we will have embarked upon a research alliance rather than a set of relationships that are unbalanced or exploitative or that ride roughshod over the rights of one group of participants (Network Goal 2). Approaches like these begin to confront what I have described elsewhere as policy research that is damaging, and replace it with a form that is epistemologically more respectful (Smyth, 2003a, 2003b, 2005a).

This leads logically into the next imperative.

Construction of an Emancipatory Knowledge Base

Developing knowledge and understanding is fundamental to what action research is all about. What makes the process unique within a collaborative action research framework is that it is done in concert with other people in ways that include them integrally and centrally in both the creation and the use of the knowledge (Network Principle 3).

When I talk about constructing an emancipatory knowledge base, what I mean is something quite different from a framework in which researchers capture knowledge to be taken away and used for their own purposes—usually for publication in obscure books or arcane journals accessible to and read by only a few privileged people. Rather, the kind of knowledge I have in mind here is distinctive in terms of its type, how it was garnered, who has access to it, how it is used, and for what purposes it was gathered or used. At its essence, knowledge that is emancipatory has the quality or the effect of freeing up, discharging, releasing from constraint, or otherwise metaphorically removing strictures that have prevented individuals or groups from knowing or doing something (Network Goal 3).

Put simply, this kind of knowledge has the following features:

- It is *relevant* to the lives of the people directly involved in the action research activity
- It is developed out of the *lives and experiences* of those people

- It is written and represented in ways that are *understandable to and that can be acted upon* by those involved in its creation
- It is of *immediacy* in the way it provides the creators with ways of *making changes* aimed at improving some aspect of their lives

There are some distinct advantages inherent in emancipatory knowledge. First, as noted earlier, it removes the kind of naked exploitation that can occur in other forms of research, where something is taken away from one group (insiders) by another group (outsiders), to be used for a purpose that is not directly of benefit to the former. When this occurs, moral questions are raised. Second, because collaborative action research invests "users" to some degree (in concert with university researchers) as co-creators of knowledge, then there is a significant aspect of empowerment or up-skilling involved. This occurs as less experienced researchers (usually, in this case, schoolteachers) learn in situ from more experienced researchers (usually university people) in ways that leave behind a modicum of skill that was not there in the beginning. This can be of significant value to those who are the direct beneficiaries (Network Principle 4). Third, what is also carried along in this process—and is often dismissed in other forms of research as mere "context"—is the history of how things came to be the way they are, and what is required to change them. This can be crucial knowledge in instances where similar attempts might be made in the future by insiders without access to outside expertise. In this sense, what is occurring is a political process in that it invests people with the agency and the capacity to take a measure of control over their lives that was denied them previously.

In this context, the kinds of questions university researchers must consider include

- Who benefits from the knowledge constructed?
- Who is included and who is excluded from the process?
- How are things materially better, and for whom, as a consequence?
- How does this knowledge invest benefits in the least advantaged?

Clearly, then, the kind of knowledge produced in and through collaborative action research has important implications for who has the power and the legitimacy to interpret, intervene in, or interrupt educational practice. This brings us back to the matter of critical engagement, with which this chapter commenced, and reopens the question of who has the right to speak about matters educational, something that is coming increasingly under threat of authoritarian control.

Vigorous Pursuit of Academic Freedom

None of what has been presented in this chapter in relation to collaborative action research is in any way intended to imply that university researchers are losing their right to actively pursue academic freedom as a consequence of collaboration with school-based practitioners. Indeed, the threat to academic freedom comes from a quite different quarter, namely from government pressure for so-called "evidence-based" or "scientific" approaches to educational research.

The kinds of questions raised for university researchers in this chapter revolve around goals of collaborative action research that are closely aligned with the unfettered pursuit of discovery, integration, application, and wider engagement involved in making knowledge public—ideals that have been argued for so forcefully by Boyer (1990, 1996) in his mission to recast universities (Network Goal 6). What has happened since Boyer, however, is a quite contrary attempt to manipulate, coerce, and direct universities along a very different path—one labeled by Erickson (2005) as "a dangerous [form] of social engineering" (p. 4). Erickson makes his point by referring to the U.S. Department of Education's recently established "clearinghouse that will tell you what works—and only evidence derived from randomized field trials will be reported by that clearinghouse" (p. 8).

According to Erickson, the U.S. government, through the Department of Education, is promulgating a massive, delusional, deceptive, and highly selective fabrication of the relationship between educational research and the conditions necessary for educational improvement (Network Goal 6). This is occurring through a dual strategy. First, there is widespread denigration and disparagement of educational research and practice, especially of the action research kind. Second, a preferred parallel construction is being posited as to how educational improvement ought to be occurring through following the supposedly more rigorous and objective field of "real science" of the kind enacted in medical research and practice. The way this latter figment is being sustained is through resort to false claims and inappropriate parallels. Erickson and Gutierrez (2002) point to the U.S. Department of Education's Strategic Plan for 2002–2007:

> Unlike medicine, agriculture, and industrial production, the field of education operates largely on the basis of ideology and professional

consensus. As such, it is subject to fads and is incapable of the cumulative progress that follows from the application of the scientific method and from the systematic collection and use of objective information in policy making. We will change education to make it an evidence-based field. . . . [T]he Department will create and regularly update an online data base of scientifically rigorous research on what works in education. (U.S. Department of Education, quoted on p. 22)

According to Erickson and Gutierrez (2002), singular reliance on narrowly focused experimentally derived causal explanations of educational program effectiveness as the supposed gold standard is a fanciful oversimplification and misrepresentation of how things actually work in the scientific and medical worlds (Network Goal 1). As they put it, scientific practice is far less predictable and certain than we are led to believe, and over many years, real scientists have been shown to be:

anything but disinterested and canonically rational. In their daily practice they are passionate and argumentative, profoundly selective in their attention to evidence, and aesthetic in drawing conclusions from it. The actual "culture of science" . . . is far from the white coat image that appears to the layperson. The accumulation of knowledge in actual science is not at all continuous—it moves by fits and starts. Real science is not about certainty but about uncertainty. (p. 22)

Erickson and Gutierrez (2002) further claim that what is going on here with respect to leveraging educational research in this direction has more to do with wishing to give "the appearance of rigor in educational research rather than its actual substance" (p. 22). In other words, trying to steer educational improvement through evidence-based approaches around supposedly scientific rigor, controlled experiments, and warehousing of knowledge through exclusive and restrictive clearinghouses is a complete sham.

Pressuring educational research in this direction is totally misguided for several reasons. First, reliance on randomized experimental trials as the sole source of what allegedly works in education tells us nothing about "how or why those treatments 'work'" (Erickson & Gutierrez, 2002, p. 22). When we know nothing about how things operate educationally, when we refuse to or are prevented from listening to or taking heed of the views of insiders, practitioners, and students, then what we have is a knowledge base that is diminished to the point of being little better than "educational superstition" (p. 22). Such official zealotry and naiveté based on such huge leaps of faith are "truly alarming" (p. 22). Berliner (2002) put the extent of the problem in some perspective when he said, "The 'evidence-based practices' and 'scientific research' mentioned over 100 times in the No Child Left Behind Act of 2001 are code words for randomized experiments" (p. 18).

Second, actively excluding local effects—as occurs in evidence-based approaches—is to assume a "high fidelity implementation [that] is rare in education" (Erickson & Gutierrez, 2002, p. 21) (Network Principle 3). In other words, it does not matter how much we try to counter the supposed limitations of the "real world" through the most faithful implementation of causal data packaged into the most structured educational improvement programs. Our unwarranted optimism will be doomed because of a totally false premise. In the medical world, from whence evidence-based practices come, "contingent circumstances" continually operate to confute and confound the conclusions of experimental studies "because of the enduring, embarrassing presence of locally constructed social facts (e.g. that many patients do not follow the prescribed medical regime: they don't take their pills or do their exercises)" (p. 23). To draw the educational parallel here, teachers have enormous veto power in terms of what they can do behind the closed door of the classroom (Network Principle 3). Finally, in education as well as in medicine, we have no way of guarding against the many unintended and undesirable side effects—that is, guarding against "premature conclusions about 'what works' in the short term . . . [that] can provide false warrants for the educational equivalent of thalidomide" (p. 23). Put most simply, the short-term press for raised achievement scores may end up producing untold future educational damage.

The intriguing question that comes to mind in all of this is, Why are we having evidence-based approaches inflicted upon educational research and educational practice, and what forces are actively holding this perspective in place? In a related vein, Why have university researchers become so compliant in having their academic freedom eroded? These are complex questions to which there are no simple answers. Unquestionably, a major part of the explanation lies in the way that as societies and as citizens we have allowed ourselves to become mesmerized (perhaps even traumatized) by the political spectacle constructed by political elites around applying corporate, military, mechanical, and medical models to the solution of complex and intractable educational questions. In the process, we have allowed ourselves to be seduced by supplicant media into believing that the only way we can operate educationally is as compliant consumers—exercising choice, demanding high standards, insisting upon value for money through accountability schemes, being assured of quality, and generally allowing schools to be regulated by the market. Not surprisingly, the educational intelligentsia has been co-opted, silenced, and marginalized. There has been no public debate about the virtues or otherwise of evidence-based approaches to research over forms like collaborative action research. Instead of being subject to robust debate, educational matters have been presented to us as if they were settled and there is no other way of thinking about the issues.

Effectively, what is occurring is that academic freedom is being closed down, and one of the few public spaces within which we can pursue real forms of educational research capable of informing us of the complexities of what occurs in schools is being eliminated. In the process, avenues for constructing viable and meaningful programs for school and classroom improvement (Network Goal 6) are disappearing.

CONCLUSION

One of the distressing consequences of not listening to the key actors in schools (such as teachers and students) can be graphically illustrated in the extent of alienation, disaffection, disengagement, violence, and premature termination of schooling being experienced by an unacceptably large number of young people (National Research Council, 2004; Smyth, 2005b; Smyth & Hattam, 2004; Smyth & McInerney, 2007; Smyth et al., 2000)—with all of the social, emotional, and economic consequences that flow from that. What is becoming labeled in the United States as the "silent epidemic" of "dropping out" of school (Bridgeland, Dilulio, & Morison, 2006) is finally but belatedly being recognized at the policy and political levels (National Governors Association, 2007). What remains to be seen is whether the political will, imagination, and courage exist to acknowledge that the official current research and policy settings are having disastrous effects on young people, and that ideas contained in books like this one provide the desperately needed alternative.

I must add a final comment, if I can be allowed a little optimistic license. The kind of recuperation, repair, and rejuvenation required for schools is one that coalesces around research in which university action researchers collaborate with teachers in schools as reflective and critical practitioners. In the process, schools become the kind of reinvented, ethically vibrant, and active sites of socially just educational inquiry we all desperately need them to be, formed around democratic relationships and a new paradigm embedded in students' and teachers' voices. The crucial issue, as Fals-Borda and

Rahman (1991) perceptively put it, is to acknowledge that social change is possible only when people are involved in generating knowledge about the conditions of their lives and are helped to see how that knowledge can be used to change the situation (Network Principles 1 and 2 and Goal 1).

It is an intriguing question as to which fantasy will win out in the end—the realistic, ethical, and collaborative one I have been arguing for here, or the fictional, ineffectual, and deeply damaging one we are bogged down in at the moment.

PART II

The School's Role

CHAPTER 5

Characteristics of More and Less Successful Action Research Programs

Stephen P. Gordon, Suzanne M. Stiegelbauer, and Julie Diehl

Steve Gordon coordinated the School Improvement Network,
Suzanne Stiegelbauer was a research consultant with the Network,
and Julie Diehl was a Network research assistant.

SCHOOL IMPROVEMENT LITERATURE often looks for common features among schools showing growth. Harris's (2002) findings on common components of improving schools included the following 10 areas: vision-building, extended leadership, selecting the school improvement program to fit the school, a focus on students, multilevel interventions (school-level, teacher-level, and classroom-level), instructionally driven programs, internal and external forces for change, investment in teaching, inquiry-led improvement, and building professional communities (within and outside of school). Common themes from the literature on improving disadvantaged schools include a focus on teaching and learning, leadership, creating an information-rich environment, creating a positive school culture, building a learning community, continuous professional development, involving parents, external support, and resources (Muijs, Harris, Chapman, Stoll, & Russ, 2004).

Building professional learning communities through school coalitions is one frequently used strategy to achieve school improvement. The Coalition of Essential Schools, begun by Ted Sizer in the early 1980s, helped high schools determine what was essential at their own school to create a program of improvement specific to that school (Sizer, 1986). The League of Professional Schools, started by Carl Glickman in the early 1990s, focused on using shared governance, action research, and an instructional focus to help schools create a plan for self-improvement (Lunsford, 1995).

ACTION RESEARCH

Action research was introduced by Kurt Lewin in 1946 to "denote a pioneering approach toward social research which combined generation of theory with changing the social system through the researcher acting on or in the social system" (Susman & Evered, 1978, p. 586). When implemented effectively, action research can "change the social system in schools and other education organizations so that continual formal learning is both expected and supported" (Calhoun, 2002, p. 18).

Although there are various models of action research, most models involve a cycle with several phases, including identifying the problem, gathering data to better understand the problem, developing an action plan aimed at solving the problem, implementing the plan, and gathering data to assess progress and revise the plan as necessary. Questions to be answered when implementing action research can include the following:

- What research issue should we choose? Why?
- What information do we need? What are the sources of this information?
- What data collection techniques will we use?
- Who is going to take part in the project? How much time will the people need to devote?
- How much work will be involved?
- What roles can each member of the team take on?
- How much time will be dedicated to the planning, the collection of information, and the individual and joint analysis?
- On which groups will we center the observation? Why?
- How are we going to exchange information?
- Who will have access to the information?
- When will reports be created? How will they be circulated?
- How will we inform other members of the educational community about our research work, and how are we going to collect and reflect on their suggestions? (adapted from Bello, 2006, p. 17)

This list of questions is a starting point for many schools to think about the process of action research.

Action research can be beneficial to schools and teachers in many ways. Glanz (1998) notes seven benefits, including creating a system-wide school improvement mind-set, enhancing decision-making, promoting reflection, committing to continuous improvement, creating a positive school climate, impacting directly on practice, and empowering teachers and schools.

ACTION RESEARCH NETWORKS

To assist schools using action research as a vehicle for school improvement, several universities have developed action research networks. Schools that belong to these networks become partners not only with the universities that organize the networks but also with the other schools within the networks. Leadership teams from schools that belong to networks typically attend network meetings to participate in professional development activities as well as to share plans, successes, problems, and possible solutions with other schools. Additionally, networks assign consultants to provide on-site support to individual schools (Calhoun & Allen, 1994; Sagor, 1991). The School Improvement Network described in the Introduction is an example of such a network. The principles, goals, organization, and support provided by the network are discussed in the first chapter. This remainder of this chapter will focus on a comparison of action research at different Network schools.

A CROSS-CASE COMPARISON:
THREE LEVELS OF SUCCESS

To document the progress of the Network schools during the first two years of action research, we conducted case studies of each school's action study, then carried out a cross-case comparison (Gordon, Stiegelbauer, & Diehl, 2006). Despite the fact that each school volunteered for the Network, agreed to the same Network goals and principles, used the same action research model, and received the same types of Network support, we found wide variation in school commitment to and implementation of action research. Based on their action research process and effects, we classified each of the schools into one of three categories: *high performance schools, coasters,* and *wheel spinners.* Here we will describe schoolwide action research within each of these three categories.

High Performance Schools

The principals' leadership was critical to the success of action research in the high performance schools. These principals were democratic leaders who provided strong support for their teachers and for action research. They provided time for the leadership team and other groups to meet on action research. They also arranged for professional development sessions on the school's focus area. The principals made resources and materials needed to conduct action research available to teachers. They made it clear that the action research was a high priority and kept it on the front burner by talking about it during faculty meetings and discussing it informally with small groups working on different aspects of the action research. One teacher described her principal's direct involvement in action research:

> She has spearheaded a lot of these discussions and concerns and she's very instrumental . . . putting articles in our box . . . "read this and get back to me and tell me what you think of this," or "read this article and share it with your grade level and get with me."

Beyond the direct support they provided, these principals distributed action research leadership throughout the school community. The fostering of teacher leadership began with the action research leadership teams. The principals treated teachers on the leadership teams as co-leaders of action research, as described by one teacher on a leadership team:

> When we meet as a group it's almost like the leadership role is gone. We're all equal group members and that I truly appreciated because it makes me feel like, "OK, I have a purpose on this team it's equal to everyone else's purpose on this team."

Beyond the action research leadership team, a variety of other groups in each of the high performance schools were involved in the action research. These groups included grade-level teams, content-area teams, vertical teams, study groups, and so on. Coordinators of these various groups also were considered leaders of action research, greatly expanding the circle of leadership in each school.

Finally, schoolwide processes embedded in the action research—processes such as collaborative decision-making, presentations to the faculty on classroom application of new instructional strategies, and peer coaching—allowed many more teachers to take leadership roles and ultimately led to a "collective leadership" of the action research. This developmental movement toward collective leadership was not an accident, but rather a strategy of the principals in the high performance schools. One principal stated, "This whole process . . . it's really empowered all of us to be leaders on this campus. . . . Our project is letting teachers be leaders . . . so, you know, when you talk about leadership there are many different levels."

Each of the Network schools was asked to select a single focus area for action research during its first year of participation. The high performance schools sought input from the school community in the selection of their focus areas. Each of these schools used a variety of strategies to gather input, including review of student performance data, small-group discussions, whole-school discussions, surveys, and the nominal group technique. A survey used by one school, for example, included the single question "What is the one area of focus that you believe would make the most impact on student achievement?" Discussions on what a school's focus area should be tended to go back and forth between small-group and whole-school discussions until a focus area was agreed upon by consensus.

Once a focus area was selected, all of the schools in the study addressed a common problem: how to get organized for action research. All of the Network schools, including the high performance schools, had considerable difficulty organizing for action research. Although a format for initiating action research had been provided by the sponsoring university (gather data on the focus area, engage in reflective dialogue on the data, identify improvement objectives, develop an action plan and an evaluation plan), the format and examples of successful action research at other schools were insufficient to guide the schools in starting their own action research. Some of the strategies used by the high performance schools in their struggle to get organized included establishing standing committees on different aspects of the focus area, discussions with critical friends, study groups, and whole-school meetings. A principal described a school meeting to decide how to approach the focus area of improving school culture and climate:

> We did . . . almost a whole-day session where we talked about "What are the components of a positive culture and climate? What does it look like?" . . . People were sitting at tables. We had each table come up with their list of things. . . . We then took all of the things that were on the list and we tried to group them, and out of that . . . we came up with making it [the school] a safer place, building collegiality and increasing the productivity [as our objectives].

These schools eventually experienced "breakthroughs," which helped them to better understand and organize for action research. These breakthroughs were different for different schools, and included insights gained at network workshops, faculty discussions, meetings with critical friends, and reflections on readings.

Gathering and analyzing data are, of course, essential components of action research. Data are the basis of the action plan, monitoring and modification of the action plan's implementation, and evaluation of effects. One characteristic of the high performance schools was continuous gathering and analysis of data for the purpose of continuous improvement of the action research. Another characteristic of these schools was the gathering of a wide variety of data. Data were gathered on student achievement, attendance, and referrals; data on teacher performance were gathered through classroom observations and teachers' self-assessments; data on teacher, student, and parent perceptions were gathered through interviews and surveys. Data were discussed at grade-level meetings, content-area meetings, vertical meetings, and faculty meetings, and action plans were revised accordingly. In short, school improvement efforts at the high performance schools were data-driven.

The high performance schools were characterized by highly effective implementation of their action plans. Time to implement action research was a problem experienced by all network schools. However, principals in the high performance schools took steps to provide teachers with time to gather data, reflect, engage in dialogue, plan for improvement, and carry out improvement activities. One critical friend working with a high performance school discussed these schools providing "the gift of time" to teachers:

> The main issue that kept coming up from the teachers was time, time, time. But part of what the school tries to give to teachers is the gift of time, trying to find creative ways to build in time for planning and collaboration. Also to provide substitutes, but not take away from productivity by providing too many subs. Also to have the teachers generate some creative ways to use existing time.

The high performance schools took an incremental approach to implementing their action plans, starting slowly, planning carefully, and developing momentum over time. Professional development was a critical component of each school's action research. Each school used a variety of professional development formats, including study groups, workshops, peer coaching, and ongoing dialogue in small-group and whole-school sessions. Other types of professional development included book clubs, watching and discussing videos on best practice, field trips to other schools, peer observation, and demonstration lessons.

Although each high performance school had a common focus area for action research, teachers were allowed a great deal of choice regarding which aspects of the action plan they worked on and how they applied the action research in their classrooms. On the other hand, it was made clear by administrators and peers that participation in the action research was a schoolwide expectation. The action research leadership teams met on a regular basis to coordinate and monitor implementation.

A phenomenon that clearly differentiated high performance schools from other Network schools was a major expansion of action research during the second year of the program. The second year of action research saw these schools increase the number of improvement objectives, the number of participants intensively involved in action research, and the number of professional development and school improvement activities incorporated into the action research.

During the second year, multiple action research teams formed to coordinate separate action research projects. One of the principals reported that his school had expanded its school improvement efforts to include 11 action research projects, and realized subsequently that the school had actually overexpanded its action research. By the end of the second year, the school had reduced the number of action research projects to eight.

High performance schools made extensive use of the critical friends assigned to them by the sponsoring university, and found the critical friends to be helpful partners in action research. One teacher said that her school's critical friend "has been a wonderful help for us, because she brings an outside perspective." Another teacher reported that her school's critical friend "helped us stay organized and focused," and a third teacher stated, "having a critical friend gave us more direction."

Principals at the high performance schools also appreciated their critical friends. One principal described her school's friend: "She's been an incredible resource. She's done something very similar with her school as principal . . . she's given us so many resources . . . she's been very active in helping us to formulate our plans." The critical friends for each of the high performance schools were equally positive about their work with the schools, reporting that it had been a personally rewarding experience for them and had enhanced their own professional development.

The high performance schools reported a wide variety of positive effects. Administrators, teachers, and critical friends reported that the action research increased collaboration and collegiality, led to more risk-taking and experimentation, and improved teaching and learning. After two years of action research, reflective inquiry had become part of the organizational culture at these schools. One principal discussing the use of reflective inquiry stated, "That's what we do . . . that's how we do business." Another principal reported that reflective inquiry had "become a daily procedure—it's engrained." A teacher from one of the high performance schools talked about the "contagious" nature of reflective inquiry:

It's very contagious. People trying out new strategies, trying to see what's successful and not successful . . . one person gets involved and somebody else wants to try it and see how successful it is in the classroom. I think people now are more willing to open up and learn . . . and the children aren't the same.

Coasters

There were no clear differences between high performance schools and coasters during the first year of action research. At the end of Year 1, the schools that eventually would morph into these two categories were all classified as *starters*, schools that, compared with wheel spinners, had more involvement and collaboration in action research, were more effectively implementing their action plans, accepted more assistance from critical friends, and experienced more positive early effects (Gordon et al., 2006).

By the end of the second year, however, the coasters clearly were putting considerably less effort into their action research, and their research was yielding diminishing returns. Because the positive aspects of the coasters' action research during Year 1 were so similar to those of the high performance schools, we will focus here on factors that eventually slowed the coasters' progress and made their action research less successful during the second year.

Principals in the coasters were not directly involved in the day-to-day facilitation of action research, especially during the second year of the project. An observer at one school described the principal's level of involvement:

Her style is not to be hands on with them . . . her expectation is that people are following through on their deadlines and their components of the project. But she is definitely not walking around checking to see what each team is doing; she's not following up.

Principals at these schools left the details of coordinating the action research to "second change facilitators" (Hord, Rutherford, Huling-Austin, & Hall, 1987). For example, in one school an assistant principal worked closely with teachers; in another school the critical friend did a great deal of coordination. Because of retirement or reassignment, however, the coasters' strongest second change agents were not present during Year 2 of the coasters' action research, when the intensity and quality of the action research diminished.

Another factor that eventually hampered the coasters' action research was the lack of a clear focus or a changing focus. One coaster, a highly innovative school, was already implementing or planning a number of improvement programs when it joined the Network. The school converted many of these programs into action research projects, planned for additional action research efforts, and attempted to integrate all of its projects under a common school improvement goal. The leadership team had the responsibility for assisting all of the action research teams. This was especially difficult for teachers on the leadership team, all of whom were on their own action research teams; they had difficulty finding time to work with the other teams. One teacher-leader stated, "Everyone has so much on their plate. I mean despite our leadership's reassurance that this wouldn't be extra work, it was." By the second year of the project, some of the action research projects had been discontinued and the others had achieved varying levels of success. An observer commented:

> *The positive of the approach was the fact the teachers could choose something of interest that would directly impact their work on a daily basis . . . the downfall of doing that was some projects went well and others didn't. Some people really took it and ran with it and others didn't . . . along the way there were several times when teachers were part of a group and then they dropped out because they moved into something else, or the teachers [in a particular group] couldn't find a common ground. You know, it sounded good in the beginning but they really couldn't figure out how to make it work. So I think it was difficult, in that with all of these different (research) areas going on, it was hard to keep them focused.*

At another coaster the principal announced at the beginning of the second year that the focus area was changing from improving communication and collegiality to improving science achievement. A teacher-leader reviewed the situation:

> *She just shared with the group that we were done [with the original focus area] and moving on. There were some protests from the teachers . . . we voiced concerns that we had made some progress but there was more to be done . . . and yes, the surveys showed improvement, that we were on our way, but we didn't feel we were there yet. But we were quickly told, "No, we have made enough progress and we're moving on." It was not up for debate or discussion.*

Although the teachers on the school's leadership team continued to facilitate action research on the new topic, many of the school's teachers had lost focus:

> *It confused a lot of teachers . . . it's hard to get people on board . . . the thought was "Why do this [if] we're going to stop again? How could you promise me we're gonna go anywhere with this, and that we're gonna go far enough to make a difference?" So it was really hard. The trust was gone.*

Another characteristic of the coasters was that they implemented action research without detailed planning. A teacher from one of the coasters put it this way: "We saw the problem and we wanted to solve it, and so . . . we just started doing the activities, but there was no plan." When one teacher was asked if there was at least an *unwritten* plan, her response was, "I believe so, but until we write it down, I don't know if we all have the same one." Although teachers in the coasters were provided time to organize and coordinate action research, some of them did not believe they were provided *sufficient* time. One teacher described this concern:

> *The planning period part is great. Yeah, we have it. But it's not always easy to get everybody together for the 45 minutes because typically . . . it's not the full 45 minutes. And 45 minutes is not enough. You never have enough time.*

Another teacher added, "Plus that's robbing us of our much needed planning and prep time and we all have plenty of things to occupy that time without action research. It's very stressful." Despite the difficulties described above, the coasters eventually submitted acceptable action plans to the Network. These plans, however, were more general than the plans submitted by the high performance schools.

Coasters gathered data periodically but did not engage in the continuous data gathering and data-based revision of action plans that characterized the high performance schools. In the words of one teacher, "I think that's where we had dropped the ball, because we were doing activity, activity, activity, but we weren't getting any data to see if it was working." The coasters tended to gather more informal, anecdotal data and less hard data than the high performance schools.

Coasters experienced initial success with implementation of their action plans, but eventually experienced problems with sustained implementation.

The coasters' leadership teams continued to attend Network workshops throughout the second year. Action research continued during the second year, but with less intensity and with diminished leader and teacher involvement. The results of action research at the coasters can best be described as mixed, with the most progress toward school improvement objectives made during the first year, and less positive results in Year 2.

Wheel Spinners

The principals at wheel spinners tended toward a directive leadership style. The wheel spinners' leadership teams relied on their principals for direction concerning the action research. During periods when direction was not forthcoming, the leadership teams engaged in little activity. In the words of one teacher, "We just kind of stay in our classrooms and do our thing." Principals from the wheel spinners were the only principals who did not regularly attend workshops on action research provided by the university.

Focus areas at the wheel spinners were selected by the principals with little or no input from teachers. In all cases, the sole reason provided by the principal for selecting a particular focus area was the need to improve student achievement in that area.

The wheel spinners had tremendous difficulty getting organized for action research. In fact, it can be argued that these schools never became fully organized for their research. The wheel spinners' action research leadership teams were not sure what their role was or how to proceed. There was little input from teachers outside the leadership teams on what action plans should consist of. Leadership teams kept discarding action plans they had begun to work on, and kept starting over from square one. A teacher at one of the wheel spinners commented on this inability to complete an action plan: "There were so many things that we didn't anticipate that we had to back up—way back—and start almost at ground zero in some areas." For wheel spinners, the curious combination of the principal's directive leadership style and the lack of principal focus on the action research greatly hindered efforts to organize for action research.

Wheel spinners gathered data on their focus area, but they tended not to collect the variety of data gathered by the high performance schools. There also was little data analysis at these schools, despite suggestions from the university consultants on how the data could be analyzed in more meaningful ways and offers by the university to assist with the analysis. Many of the data on the focus area never went beyond the action research leadership team, therefore the wider faculty had little involvement in data analysis.

Although wheel spinners eventually submitted action plans, there seemed to be little connection between the data gathered on the focus area and the action plans. Wheel spinners did not gather data to track the progress or effects of the action research.

Wheel spinners never implemented their action plans in a comprehensive manner, although some improvement activities were carried out. Compared with other Network schools, fewer teachers at the wheel spinners were involved with the action research. In the final analysis, both administrators and teachers in the wheel spinners saw implementation of their action plan as just one of several competing demands. The wheel spinners prioritized other demands as more important (or at least more urgent) than their action plans, and thus never got off the ground with the action research. It is interesting that, despite the lack of implementation, the leadership teams from the wheel spinners continued to attend the all-day Network workshops provided by the university. This indicates that the teams believed they were getting something out of the professional development sessions, and they saw at least some potential in the action research model.

During the first year of the program, despite repeated attempts to meet with the wheel spinners' action research leadership teams, the critical friends assigned to work with those schools were essentially shut out of the schools' work on action research. This created a great deal of frustration for the critical friends, who were highly committed to assisting the schools with their action research. During the second year, new critical friends—highly experienced in school-based action research—were assigned to the wheel spinners. These critical friends participated in discussions with the administrations and leadership teams, and in one case involved some teachers from a wheel spinner in a small-scale action research project. In general, however, the new critical friends were unable to facilitate wheel spinners toward the type of comprehensive schoolwide action research fostered by the Network.

Considering the fact that the action plans at the wheel spinners were neither effectively implanted nor evaluated by these schools, it is not surprising that positive effects of the action research were minimal. Compared with both high performance schools and coasters, wheel spinners reported less progress toward research objectives, less professional growth, less improvement in school culture, and less improvement of teaching and learning.

REFLECTIONS ON THE CASE STUDIES

Administration and teachers from all of the schools attended a daylong orientation before they joined the School Improvement Network at which they were provided an overview of schoolwide action research and were informed of the commitments expected of schools joining the Network. All of the schools enthusiastically became part of the Network and sent their action research leadership teams to periodic daylong workshops over a two-year period. Despite the initial commitment and ongoing professional development, some of the schools never made any significant progress on their action research, and some others coasted through the second year after making meaningful progress during the first year. On the other hand, other schools used their action research to transform their schools into the communities of inquiry that action research is intended to promote.

A university partner or support network can provide professional development, material resources, moral support, and technical assistance to schools engaging in action research. However, in the final analysis, it is up to the individual school to plan and implement action research that will lead to meaningful change in the school culture, teaching, and learning. Despite the unique nature of each schoolwide action research project, our comparative case study has provided us with some predictors of success with schoolwide action research, and some indicators of what a university partner and school can do to increase the chances of success once action research has begun.

Predictors of Success

One predictor of success is democratic school leadership. A school with a highly directive principal probably should not initiate schoolwide action research unless the principal is ready to commit to a change of leadership style. The two-way dialogue, shared decision-making, collegiality, and collaboration at the heart of schoolwide action research simply are not compatible with principal control of the action research process. One option is for principals with directive leadership styles to participate in professional development to increase their leadership flexibility prior to initiating an action research program. One of the teachers from a coaster discussed some dispositions that a principal needs to develop prior to leading action research. These include being open to dialogue, being willing to give up control, and trusting teachers to make good decisions.

Another predictor of success is a commitment from a large portion of the school community (not just a leadership team with several teachers) to engage in schoolwide action research. One way of assessing whether this commitment is present is to follow up a network orientation for leadership teams with an on-site orientation for individual schools that have expressed initial interest in action research. The entire school community can then take a democratic vote on whether it wishes to participate.

A third predictor is the presence a collective school vision, and the school community's ability to conceptualize, in general terms, how school-wide action research can be used to help the school move toward that shared vision. Merely being enamored with the concept of action research does not seem to be a sufficient reason to initiate an action research program. Also, attempting to convert existing school improvement efforts into action research projects does not seem to work. Rather, the school must have a vision of where it wants to go, recognize significant change that must occur if it is to move toward that vision, and view schoolwide action research as the primary means for achieving that change. Action research is a long-term, labor-intensive process, and it does not fare well if it is seen as one of several competing priorities or, worse yet, as an add-on to a school agenda that is already full. If schoolwide action research is to be successful, it must be viewed from the beginning as the primary vehicle for school improvement.

A fourth predictor of success is an infrastructure, or at least a commitment to build an infrastructure, that will provide time and opportunities for teachers to engage in data gathering, data analysis, planning, improvement activities, and most importantly, dialogue about the action research. Although time was an issue for all of the Network schools, a common characteristic of the high performance schools was frequent small-group and whole-school meetings to complete tasks and engage in dialogue related to the action research.

Increasing the Chances of Success

Following are recommendations for increasing the chances that action research supported by a university-based action research network will take root and grow within individual schools.

1. Professional development for leadership teams offered by the university should include special emphasis on shared decision-making, integrating action research with the school's vision, organizing for action research, data gathering and analysis, planning action research, implementing action research, and the long-term goal of creating a culture of inquiry.
2. Although a partner university or action research network cannot provide the same professional development to each entire network school that it provides to the leadership teams, at least one on-site whole-school professional development session

should be provided by outside experts early in the program. This session should provide the entire school community with an overview of the purpose, principles, and process of action research.

3. Regular visits to all participating schools by critical friends assigned to those schools is essential. The critical friend provides moral support, critical feedback, and technical assistance to the school. It is important that the critical friend have expertise in action research and school improvement.

4. During the first year of action research the school should have a single focus area, with all school groups working on various aspects of that focus area. If, eventually, different teams develop separate action research projects, the number of those projects should be limited and all projects should be related directly to the school's vision and coordinated in a manner that will move the school toward its vision.

5. School leaders should involve as many members of the school community as possible in the action research. Although an action research leadership team including a majority of teachers is necessary to coordinate the process, action research that stays in the hands of the leadership team will not succeed. School leaders need to keep action research on the front burner, discussing it regularly with various groups and at faculty meetings and supporting it by providing participants with time and other resources necessary for successful implementation.

6. Ongoing data gathering and analysis, collaborative decision-making, and reflective dialogue are three critical aspects of schoolwide action research that need to be priorities for administrators and teachers.

7. Schools should gather a variety of data (rather than a single measure such as standardized test scores) as a basis for determining the focus area, designing an action plan, monitoring implementation of the plan, and assessing progress. Analysis and discussion of data are as important as data gathering, thus regular opportunities for both small-group and whole-school review of data should be provided.

8. It seems that successful action research programs gradually increase in complexity, adding new improvement objectives, new participants, and new curricular and instructional innovations over time. This expansion, if it is incremental, can keep

the action research process dynamic and foster continuous school improvement.

9. Administrators and teachers involved in action research should be encouraged to share their research with a larger education community, such as other schools in the district, other members of an action research network, or at regional or national conferences. Action research can be shared nationally and internationally by placing electronic portfolios documenting action research on the World Wide Web. Schools involved in action research should celebrate their accomplishments both privately and publicly.

10. The most positive outcome for the high performance schools was the evidence that the administrators and teachers in these schools had made reflective inquiry a part of their school's culture and their own professional lives. The outcomes at these schools suggest that the long-term goal of action research should not be to simply meet short-term improvement goals but to develop communities of reflective inquiry with the capacity for continuous renewal.

CONCLUSION

Action research can be a vehicle for school improvement, but schoolwide action research requires extensive internal and external support. Schools need internal support in the form of strong, democratic leadership; widespread collaboration; and time to participate in action research. Schools need external support in the form of professional development for leadership teams, networking with other schools engaged in action research, and on-site consultation. Also, schools need to continuously revise action research and expand participation in action research if it is to result in long-term, continuous school improvement. This is a critical finding if we accept the idea that the ultimate purpose of schoolwide action research is to create communities of reflective inquiry with the capacity for continuous self-renewal.

CHAPTER 6

Readiness for Collaborative Action Research

Marla W. McGhee and Michael Boone

---

*Marla McGhee and Michael Boone were critical friends
for the School Improvement Network.*

IN THIS CHAPTER we discuss selected attributes of schools that are *ready* to engage in collaborative action research as well as describe the characteristics of schools that are not, with a particular focus on the challenges faced by high schools and large campuses. Moreover, we discuss how schools can move toward readiness for action research and school improvement. We close the chapter by sharing a vignette and lessons learned in a unique multiyear school improvement initiative, specifically describing the readiness barriers experienced by one of the high schools that participated in the School Improvement Network.

RECOGNIZING AND UNDERSTANDING READINESS FOR ACTION RESEARCH

Numerous factors in the school environment can be linked to readiness for collaborative work and organizational growth through action research, such as faculty commitment to student learning, a process for collective decision-making, and a team approach for leading and facilitating action research initiatives (Calhoun, 1994). Below we highlight several related factors that contribute to readiness, including sharing and nurturing leadership, leaders who follow, and an environment conducive to innovation.

Sharing Leadership and Nurturing Teamwork

"Keeping good teachers should be one of the most important agenda items for any school leader" (Darling-Hammond, 2003, p. 7). When principals and assistant principals establish professional rapport with teachers and sustain positive working conditions and circumstances for them, it is much more likely that teachers will remain in the profession and students and the school will prosper. Because good teachers tend to be attracted to schools where they know they will be supported, respected, and appreciated, campus-level leaders who devote time and focused energy to nurturing teamwork and sharing leadership help to promote the readiness of their school to engage in collaborative improvement efforts. "Effective teachers constitute a valuable human resource for schools—one that needs to be treasured and supported" (p. 7). Moreover, because school leadership is actually "stretched over the school's social and situational contexts" (Spillane, Halverson, & Diamond, 2001, p. 23), promoting shared responsibility around issues such as establishing student learning goals and making critical campus decisions simply makes good sense. This may be especially true when it comes to crafting and implementing effective campus improvement initiatives. As Darling-Hammond (2003), Lieberman and Miller (1992), and others have shown over time, team structures and reflective practice groups have "demonstrated the power of collegial networks and partnerships" (Donaldson, 2006, p. 30). Thus, in schools where teachers are recognized, practicing leaders, team-based inquiry is a natural next step, made easier if a culture of shared leadership and collaboration already exists.

Leaders Who Follow

Related to the issue of teamwork and shared organizational responsibility is the readiness concept of leader as follower. Depending on the endeavor, a campus leader's expertise may be best used at the group or collective level (Spillane et al., 2001). Additionally, leaders who are able to successfully take a place inside the team or alongside the group serve as powerful models for their professional peers.

> At the core of this dance is the leader's professional and personal relationship with staff members. How principals . . . respond to this . . . establishes whether trust, openness, and personal affirmation will be the rule in the relationship or whether it will be marked by domination, required compliance, and fear. (Donaldson, 2006, p. 37)

Principals and assistant principals who practice cooperation and active group participation—allowing others to take the lead—do much to help overcome naturally occurring leader–follower tensions. This idea is paralleled and reinforced in the National Staff Development Council's (NSDC) standards for practice and implementation, which suggest that a principal with the highest level of performance participates in decision-making committees as "another member of the group" and encourages others to take leadership roles during meetings (Roy & Hord, 2003, p. 95). Therefore, in schools where principals and assistant principals model followership by willingly and effectively working alongside teachers, collaborative action research is more likely to take hold quickly and more apt to succeed.

An Environment Conducive to Innovation

A third readiness factor related to the promotion of collaborative inquiry is a school culture or environment that invites innovation and risk-taking. An array of issues can contribute to shaping the professional culture in the school. Consider, for example, the role and influence of the leader. When campus leaders embrace or, better yet, model change and innovation, others in the organization will likely take notice. Zimmerman (2006) argues that if the principal expects teachers to take risks, he or she must also be open to new learning and behaviors, even if engaging in the learning may potentially expose weaknesses. Such modeling is powerful in creating a culture where trying new things becomes part of the way we do business.

Boosting teacher confidence and self-efficacy while reducing professional stress can also shape innovative practices within a school (Fullan, 2001a; Goleman, Boyatzis, & McKee, 2002). When teachers feel comfortable trying new methods or strategies, knowing that the risk of penalty or sanction for a failed attempt is low, their willingness to participate is positively impacted. Likewise, teachers with high self-confidence and efficacy tend to challenge and motivate themselves, and shape their own actions by envisioning and then pursuing a path to success (Zimmerman, 2006).

As Rowan and Miller (2007) note, "organization theorists have argued that risk aversion can be mitigated by developing an organizational culture that facilitates worker autonomy and discretion and that overtly rewards risk taking and innovation" (p. 257). In schools where teachers and staff are openly praised or celebrated for trying new or different skills at whole-school meetings, during departmental gatherings, and in one-to-one interactions, enthusiasm for this professional way of life is enhanced and encouraged. "This recognition can be as simple as the principal sharing positive feedback about the school's progress at faculty meetings or giving personal notes to staff members who have contributed to the effort" (Zimmerman, 2006, p. 245). So, when principals and assistant principals model adult learning by taking on educational innovations themselves, and encourage or reward risk-taking and well-reasoned experimentation without fear of retribution, they help to promote an environment of readiness.

IDENTIFYING AND GRAPPLING WITH BARRIERS TO SCHOOL IMPROVEMENT

Just as there are factors that enable readiness for collaborative inquiry and improvement, there are also recognized barriers that stand in the way of reform efforts. In the sections below, we identify and present several stumbling blocks: organizational issues, challenges to developing and using teacher-leaders, and the complexity of high school improvement. In the discussion of high schools, we elaborate in depth on a range of ideas in the belief that what we have learned from past and present practice can positively inform our work for the future.

Organizational Barriers to Change

Scholars and practitioners have long recognized that public schools are difficult organizations to change. Sarason (1990), reflecting on more than a decade of school reform efforts, notes the seeming intractability of public schools and predicts the ultimate failure of school reform unless the tactics of reformers change dramatically. Sarason argues that the outside-in and top-down approach of traditional school reform initiatives has failed and urges a change to an inside-out and bottom-up approach to changing schools. The problem with the hierarchical method is that it fails to impact core assumptions and structures of the school—the culture. Reforms imposed from the outside ignore the power of organizational culture in shaping the assumptions and beliefs of teachers, motivating behavior, affecting the ability of principals to lead others, and influencing the way important decisions are made in the school. Imposed reform may change some of the formal organizational aspects of a school but leave its culture intact.

As an example of how the culture and structures of the organization can impact behavior, consider what Donaldson (2006) calls the "conspiracy of busyness." By this, he means the ways in which the culture and structure of the school work against change and thwart even the best intentions of leaders. "The apparent failure of imposed restructuring and reform solutions," Donaldson writes, "stands as frustrating proof of this point" (p. 14).

Several structural elements impede school improvement. The first of these is a lack of time for teachers to plan and organize change. Schools by and large are designed for teaching students, not for adult collaboration and work. Donaldson (2006) notes that teachers spend the vast majority of their time in direct interaction with students; planning lessons; conferring with students, other teachers, and parents; and eating lunch. They are largely unavailable for other types of activity, including collaborative work that would lead to school improvement. The typical school schedule also leaves little time for principal leadership. Moreover, when principals and teachers do converse, conversations are limited to minutes carved out of an already full day and conducted in a fairly random and haphazard manner. Third, when formal meetings do occur they are typically one of two types: whole-faculty meetings and committee or team meetings. Donaldson refers to these types of meetings as "suboptimal leadership events" (p. 18) in which participation is irregular, that extend the school day, that happen too infrequently to sustain continuity from one meeting to the next, and in which the quality of interaction is minimal. Whole-faculty and team meetings often fail to provide sufficient quality time for change leadership to be exercised.

School size creates other barriers that constrict opportunities for change. Bigger campuses and student bodies require larger faculties, resulting in fewer opportunities for meaningful one-to-one interactions. Large schools require a more hierarchical structure simply to function, which restricts the choice of available decision-making processes that can be implemented. School size also impacts students. Uncomfortable in large schools, students find ways of making them feel smaller (Daniels, Bizar, & Zemelman, 2001). Particularly in high schools, where thousands of students may be enrolled, unofficial but influential subgroups or cliques with which students can identify and from which they derive a sense of identity seem to flourish. These subgroups can interfere with student learning and stymie the building of a sense of community in the school. In large schools the obstacles both students and adults face in developing a sense of belonging, working collaboratively, or even maintaining communication are formidable.

We can draw several conclusions about the barriers organizational structure places in the way of school improvement. The first is that reform efforts that seek to personalize large schools by reducing the number of adults with whom a student interacts through the establishment of smaller learning communities, schools-within-schools, and faculty advisory programs are on the right track. Reform initiatives with these specific goals should be supported and perfected. Second, the nature of leadership in schools must be rethought. Leadership models that reflect the realities of school structures are greatly needed. Barriers can be broken when leaders and followers work together in such a way that "schools become environments that support productive work and learning for *both* children and adults" (Donaldson, 2006, p. 25). In summary, it is clear that as schools at all levels become larger and more complex organizations, the time available for planning and monitoring of improvement measures diminishes dramatically, creating barriers to meaningful and lasting collaborative reform, and requiring new forms of leadership.

Empowering Others to Lead: The Challenge of Developing and Using Teacher-Leaders

As Harris (2002) states, there are a number of factors that will prevent school improvement from taking hold: unclear goals and purposes, competing priorities, lack of support, insufficient attention to implementation, and inadequate leadership. Conversely, there are a host of reasons that school improvement efforts succeed, including a focus at the classroom level, insisting on sound implementation, collecting evaluative evidence along the way, and engaging teachers in professional dialogue and development (Harris, 2002). Although school improvement programs and projects may vary in content and approach, they share a similar theme. "Central to this philosophy is an adherence to the school as the center of change and the teacher as the catalyst for classroom change and development" (p. 29). Yet in many schools, teachers are simply not involved in thinking about, designing, or leading school-level improvement initiatives.

A 2001 task force report entitled *Leadership for Student Learning: Redefining the Teacher as Leader* states that teachers must help in exercising leadership, especially when instructional matters are at stake. However, the report goes on to say,

> As long as school leadership remains mostly top-down and hierarchical, there is little chance that teachers will ever be more than fringe players— available as a resource when called upon, but seldom directly and continuously involved in decisions of substance. (Task Force on Teacher Leadership, Institute for Educational Leadership, 2001, p. 9)

Lambert (2005) notes that schools with low or moderate leadership capacity are not likely to embrace or practice effective teacher leadership. In such schools the environment and personnel tend to be principal-dependent, lack purpose and focus, and suffer from fragmentation and polarization. According to Lovely (2005), "the concept of shared leadership is one of the most neglected elements of professional development for administrators and teachers" (p. 17).

What appears to be needed is a model that takes advantage of the opportunities the current structure provides and facilitates the emergence of informal teacher-leadership. Hord (1992) call it "facilitative leadership." The approach combines democratic leadership with the skills associated with a proficient staff development facilitator to build relationships with followers. The facilitative concept enables a principal to directly confront many of the barriers to change present in the school and to support the emergence of formal and informal leaders among teachers. As Hord describes it, facilitative leaders possess a distinct set of characteristics. They have a vision for what the school can be and are skilled in communicating that vision to teachers, staff, and students. Facilitative leaders hold a set of clearly defined educational values and model those values in the routines they create for the organization. They attend to the personal needs of teachers that arise from the daily operation of the school, especially issues surrounding instruction, supervision, or teacher difficulties with students or parents. Facilitative leaders address conflict directly and develop trust with teachers, students, and staff by holding true to their word. These leaders also model followership by working alongside others in the school community as a peer rather than a superior. Most importantly, all facilitative leaders create opportunities to expand the leadership pool within the school by actively encouraging individuals and groups of teachers to assume significant leadership roles.

A facilitative approach may be one way for principals to heed Donaldson's call for a leadership style that will overcome barriers to change in schools. Without meaningful and purposeful attention and engagement, attempts to broaden a school's leadership circle by empowering a great number of teachers into leadership roles is not likely to take place in an effective or substantive way.

Understanding the Difficulty of High School Reform

The school reform movement seems to have passed by the American high school. Compared with the fundamental changes that have impacted elementary and middle schools, high schools remain much the same as they were 30 years ago. Daniels et al. (2001) write that, as institutions, high schools are "profoundly, frustratingly intractable. They seem to shrug off all criticism, squirm out from under all indictments, and repel all changes" (p. 19). The litany of alleged failures of the high school is all too familiar. Critics point to low test scores, ballooning dropout rates, violence and disorder among students, seemingly insurmountable racial disparities in student achievement, and a general disconnect between the traditional high school curriculum and the world in which students actually live (Daniels et al., 2001). Students themselves complain that their high school coursework did not challenge them intellectually or prepare them for college or the workplace, an assessment with which their employers and professors tend to agree (Achieve, Inc., 2005). What makes high schools seemingly immune to reform is open to speculation. Some commentators point to the conservative nature of schooling itself, which renders the pace of change almost glacial; others lament the adherence to an outdated industry-derived organizational model that creates an authoritarian, hierarchical, and socially stratified institution that is no longer relevant to a highly mobile, technologically sophisticated society (Daniels et al., 2001; Sparks, 2001). Others suggest that today's earlier maturing adolescents are ill suited to an institution designed a century or more ago to serve students who were physically and socially still children (Botstein, 1997). Whatever the causes might be, the time for meaningful reform of the American high school has come.

Evaluating Past School Improvement Initiatives

Business groups, politicians, and a variety of foundations and organizations have exerted a powerful influence on the direction of high school reform in recent years. One of the most extensive approaches to high school reform from the private sector has been funded by the Bill and Melinda Gates Foundation, which since 2000 has contributed millions of dollars to projects designed to improve American high schools. Gates money supports three types of high school redesign efforts: *Model Schools*, innovative new high schools that were not in existence prior to the grant; *New Schools*, which are autonomous charter schools; and *Redesigned Schools*, existing comprehensive high schools transforming themselves into small learning communities (American Institutes for Research, 2005). Gates Foundation–funded schools tend to serve predominantly disadvantaged students who enter high school a year or more behind grade level in academic skills.

Gates-sponsored school reform projects are designed to create and sustain high schools for all students that exhibit the same "culture of learning" that characterizes the most successful high schools (Coalition of Essential Schools, 2000). This culture includes a common focus on learning for all students, high student expectations, a safe place marked by positive relationships between students and adults, time for teachers to collaborate, competency-based student promotions, and widespread use of technology for instruction. The Gates Foundation's goal is to transform troubled, low-performing high schools into places of learning "where students and adults know each other well and . . . where the professional community is collaborative and student focused" (Shear et al., 2005, p. 14). Foundation officials also believe that small school size is critical to school improvement, not as an end in itself but as a way to create a learning culture.

Evaluation of the progress made by Gates-funded projects is ongoing (American Institutes for Research, 2005; Rhodes et al., 2005; Shear et al., 2005). Much of the evaluative focus has been on new and redesigned high schools, and the results are mixed. Because these schools tend to serve mostly a disadvantaged student population that is already deficient in academic skills, "mixed results" may mean progress is being made. At the end of the evaluation period (2004), students and teachers at newly established high schools (predominantly charter schools) reported a continuing positive school culture. However, other indicators of effectiveness tended to decline slightly. Most academic progress in new schools occurs in the third year. Student achievement gains for both new and redesigned schools were reported in reading, English, and language arts but not in mathematics, where a lack of rigor in teacher assignments and student work was noted. Evaluators called for increased attention to mathematics content and instruction. Student attendance was higher in the new schools than in the redesigned schools. For both categories of schools, external factors, especially budget cuts, exacerbated efforts to preserve a positive school culture. Also, for both types of schools, the critical factor leading to success was the quality of leadership in the school. Teacher capacity and workload are problems for smaller schools. Overall, new schools seem to hold an advantage over redesigned schools in most categories of comparison, although the redesigned schools did demonstrate progress over time, especially in creating a positive school culture (Robelen, 2005).

The Gates Foundation is not alone on the high school reform scene. Quint (2006) reviewed evaluation results from studies of three "families" of comprehensive high school reform models: First Things First, Talent

Development, and Career Academies. Together, these models have been implemented in over 2,500 high schools nationally, and aspects of each program are in place in several hundred other high schools. The impact of these three models has been extensive. First Things First was installed initially in 10 high schools in Kansas City, Kansas, beginning in 1999 to serve a population made up of low-income Black and Hispanic students. Key elements of the program include the development of schoolwide, thematic, small learning communities, as well as instructional support programs for students performing below grade level. Evaluation of the program in 2006 indicated increased attendance and graduation rates, reduced dropout rates, and improved performance on state tests of reading and mathematics at the initial site, but significantly less progress at extension sites in Texas, Mississippi, and Missouri. Talent Development initiatives include such things as ninth-grade success academies, career academies, extended block schedules, and "catch-up" courses for ninth-grade students with low skills. Implemented in 1999 in Philadelphia, the program served a predominantly minority and low-income student population. Findings from the evaluation of Talent Development programs documented gains in academic course credits earned and promotion rates for ninth-graders that were sustained as students moved through high school. Career Academies is a national reform initiative dating back to 1993. There are implementation sites in California, Washington, D.C., Florida, Maryland, Pennsylvania, and Texas. Career academies include such features as schools-within-a-school, school–employer partnerships, and integrated academic and occupational curricula. Evaluation results noted higher postgraduation earnings for young men who were at medium or high risk of dropping out of school, but no impact on high school graduation rates or enrollment in postsecondary education.

In her review of the evaluation results for these three initiatives, Quint (2006) notes that although these programs failed to meet all of the high expectations of their developers and adopters, there were small gains, and even small gains can be important. Modest positive percentage changes in academic achievement or graduation rates, or lower dropout rates, actually represent improvement for hundreds of students.

Education-related groups have also joined the discussions over high school reform. Nearly every subject-matter professional group has contributed its own recommendations for reform to the debate. Organizations such as the National Council of Teachers of Mathematics, the American Association for the Advancement of Science, the National Writing Project, the National Council for the Social Studies, the National Council of the

Teachers of English, and the International Reading Association have established sets of "best practices" for the teaching of their discipline that are reflected, to some degree, in most state standards for student achievement (Zemelman, Daniels, & Hyde, 1998). Even with these compelling standards and a documented set of exemplary best practice classrooms across the United States, systematic or widespread application of these practices in high schools is far from the norm.

The National Association of Secondary School Principals (NASSP) is another major voice for high school improvement. NASSP's reform agenda in spelled out in two publications: *Breaking Ranks: Changing an American Institution* (Brown, 1996), published jointly with the Carnegie Foundation for the Advancement of Teaching, and *Breaking Ranks II: Strategies for Leading High School Reform* (National Association of Secondary School Principals, 2004), published in cooperation with the Education Alliance at Brown University. *Breaking Ranks* offers a set of recommendations to guide high school reform throughout the nation, and *Breaking Ranks II* provides principals, teachers, and parents with a set of strategies for implementing the recommendations in their schools and districts. Together the publications comprise a comprehensive approach to high school reform backed by the men and women most directly concerned with improving high schools—principals and assistant principals. Unfortunately, many campus leaders and their local communities remain unaware of this work and its potential impact on high school students and their achievement.

The American high school has been the primary target of major redesign efforts in recent years. Groups and interested individuals both inside and outside of education have raised public awareness of the need for reform and carried through with a variety of redesign initiatives. Further improvement efforts will benefit from a thorough knowledge of which past reforms have been wholly or partially successful and which have not achieved their purposes. Because action research entails a systematic review of current knowledge and experience surrounding the selected focus areas, knowing the results of past high school reform programs should prove invaluable in designing future action research.

STEPS TO PROMOTE READINESS FOR SCHOOL IMPROVEMENT

Below we offer four steps for moving toward readiness for collaborative action research aimed at school improvement. Each step offers incremental progress toward a more cooperative, site-based problem-solving environment.

Step 1: Helping Educators to Understand and Embrace the Concept of Action Research

Administrators and teachers are constantly being pressured to alleviate problems by *taking action*. Too often, though, the absence of a problem-solving process or school improvement model causes programs to be instituted without careful vetting for appropriateness and fit, resulting instead in "fixes that fail" (Senge et al., 2000). Action research is a valuable tool for the reform of high schools and for the improvement of schools of all levels. Emily Calhoun (2002) writes that action research is a process of continual inquiry designed to "inform and improve our practice as educators" (p. 18). It provides a vehicle to examine work in context, to review current research for possible solutions, to compare best practice with current practice, to develop a plan for needed changes, and to evaluate the results. Action research encourages the collection, analysis, and use of accurate student data in making decisions about instruction. It is continuous and cyclical, and contributes to a culture of continuous inquiry in the school. It is this culture of inquiry that raises action research above other school improvement initiatives (Calhoun, 2002).

Action research is the combination of three separate but necessary processes: action, research, and participation (Greenwood & Levin, 2007). Participation is the key ingredient, for without it, the research may prove valuable but it is not *action* research. Action research empowers participants to take control of their own situations by studying the circumstances in which they live or work, by gathering and analyzing data, by developing a solution to a perceived problem, and by implementing and evaluating the solution. Participation "is not the cause of a good AR process; it is an instrument of a broader process of co-generative knowledge creation, action design, and evaluation" (Greenwood & Levin, 2007, p. 256). Embedded in an authentic action research cycle, participation is empowerment. To promote action research, campus leaders should consider the following:

- Making site visits to schools currently conducting action research
- Conducting a book study on action research with a group of interested volunteers
- Forming action research study groups or teams to support initial classroom and school-based inquiry projects

Given adequate administrative and organizational support, leadership will emerge from among teachers and others engaged in action research, the social system of the school will begin to change, and the door to readiness and meaningful reform will be opened.

Step 2: Start Small

Long-term, comprehensive improvement projects can be challenging and overwhelming. Understandably, setbacks and performance dips will occur along any long-range implementation path, causing participants to lose sight of their ultimate improvement goal. To deal with these potential problems, change leaders should focus on short-term achievements along the way.

> After one semester of implementing some of the changes, the building might have experienced fewer disciplinary referrals, fewer course failures, and/or increased attendance. By collecting and analyzing similar data, these important short-term wins can be celebrated, if only in some small way. . . . Much-deserved celebrations can create the energy and motivation necessary to persevere in the long haul. (Zimmerman, 2006, p. 245)

As Zimmerman notes, acknowledging short-term victories and accomplishments can make staying committed to a long-term improvement plan more manageable. Moreover, fashioning plans that initially target a specific group (grade level, department, division, or discipline) rather than the entire campus increases the likelihood of success.

Step 3: Pilot for Progress

Related to the issue of small-scale or short-range change is the concept of piloting innovations or interventions prior to fully implementing them. A primary tenet of the Accelerated Schools comprehensive improvement model (Levin, 1986) is systematic problem-solving using an inquiry process that includes piloting possible solutions, observing what works, and making appropriate adjustments before moving forward with larger scale implementation. In this school improvement model, once areas of need are identified, cadres form to target and study specific areas of concern. After data have been carefully examined, and the literature consulted for guidance and possible solutions, each cadre initiates a pilot program to "test" their proposed intervention plan. Based on the results of the pilot program, each study cadre makes recommendations to the larger school community about possible next steps. This approach allows schools to move carefully, yet purposefully, toward addressing school-based issues or problems. So, like the use of smaller scale initiatives, piloting possible solutions promotes readiness for larger, more comprehensive improvement measures.

Step 4: Use a Second Change Facilitator

When it comes to readiness for engaging in collaborative action research the issue of who leads or initiates a change can be a critical consideration. In instances where the formal leader—the principal, for example—is not the best choice for a change leader, or where the primary leader cannot or will not lead, a second change facilitator may be necessary.

A study conducted in the early 1990s targeting principals and assistant principals in central Texas reinforced this concept (McGhee, 1992). In some of the schools studied, the most effective change leader was not the principal, but an assistant principal. This was particularly noticeable in the schools where the principal was identified by the faculty (via the Change Facilitator Style Questionnaire) as a Responder-change leader (Hall & Hord, 2006). In this study, a Responder-style administrator, least effective on the change-leadership continuum, was often complemented or assisted by an Initiator (most effective in impacting change) vice principal.

> Of the Initiator administrators identified, most were assistant principals. This indicates that in schools where there are effective principal co-workers, the assistant performs a shared role in facilitating change, while on campuses with an ineffective principal, the Initiator assistant serves as the primary change agent. This finding suggests that change efforts might best be orchestrated and accomplished by a team or through a shared approach, tapping into the usefulness of secondary change facilitators. (McGhee, 1992, p. 96)

A variety of scholars have stressed the importance of secondary change leaders in helping site-level research and innovation to take hold. Practically speaking, the complex nature of schools requires that others (besides the principal) get involved in continuous improvement efforts. Engaging and empowering secondary change leaders from both the administrative and the teaching ranks is a move toward readiness and a step in the right direction.

NETWORK SCHOOL VIGNETTE:
THE RIGORS, RESPONSIBILITIES, AND CHALLENGES
OF OPENING A NEW HIGH SCHOOL—LESSONS OF
READINESS FROM ONE SCHOOL'S EXPERIENCE

As noted earlier, readiness factors can either enhance or impede the success of collaborative action research endeavors. Additionally, contextual and situational circumstances such as those presented in the following vignette can impact the success of schoolwide action research.

Struggles of a New School and a New Leader

The first year of Smith High's involvement as a Network school was its opening year of operation. With new faculty and staff and a student body made up of ninth- and tenth-graders, the school was striving—and struggling, in some ways—to create its campus and community culture. When the principal reflected back on the year, she noted that prior to the opening of the campus, she was filled with enthusiasm for the work and could see herself serving as this school's principal for many years to come. But, as that first year wore on, she admitted there were days when she wondered if she would successfully navigate even one year. The work at times was overpowering, overbearing, and overwhelming. The fact that this bright leader with an extensive background in campus-level and district-wide professional development, and a Ph.D. in educational leadership from a prominent university, doubted her long-term ability to lead was clear indication of the daunting nature of the leadership role. She reported long and unrelenting hours on the job and away from her family with myriad instructional challenges, including the performance of students on state-mandated standardized assessments and addressing unsatisfactory course failure rates. Although she was building a talented faculty and an able leadership team who were capable of accomplishing much together, the difficulty of setting up and establishing the operation of a new campus made it hard to focus on tasks such as collaborative action research.

District Stability and Leadership

A second contextual factor for this school and its leadership was the issue of district-level administration, guidance, and support. Just prior to the beginning of the school year, the superintendent of schools was hired away by an educational organization located in a nearby city, leaving the rapidly growing and increasingly diverse district with no top executive leadership. Rather than conducting an immediate superintendent search, the district's Board of Trustees decided instead to appoint a three-member panel of high-ranking administrators to handle superintendency-type duties for the school district. The uncertainty and instability created by these circumstances impacted every campus in the district in some manner, including the recently opened high school. Knowing who to contact for what was constantly in question and made this time of district transition an additional challenge for the new school, its leaders, faculty, and staff. Where some may have viewed this circumstance (a vacant superintendency) as the ultimate opportunity to practice unfettered site-based decision-making and a chance to exercise organizational freedom, the new high school campus and new high school principal seemed to need something different. As Cuban (2007) espouses, one of the most productive arrangements for schools is a healthy combination of grassroots energy and action with district-level resources, guidance, and support. In this instance, a better balance of the two would probably have been beneficial.

Making a Productive External Match

An issue of note that further stalled the performance of this high school campus in the Network improvement project was external circumstance created when university personnel working with the initiative assigned the original set of critical friends to work with this school. Although most of the Network schools were paired with full-time university faculty members to serve as external mentors, others were matched with able and energetic doctoral students. Some of the doctoral student–school relationships flourished and were among the most productive in the Network. Yet, for this campus, the pairing never gelled. Even after multiple offers by the two assigned doctoral students to meet with the principal and the leadership team, the relationship and potential support from these critical friends did not develop. At the final network meeting of the first year of the initiative, school representatives asked for a change in critical friends assignment. Taking cues from the mentoring literature, noting that the most productive relationships are sometimes established and fostered by the mentee rather than assigned by a third party, the school's request for a change in critical friends assignment was granted. The school asked to work with a specific full-time university professor, so the shift in assignment was established. This experience stands as an important reminder that compatibility and fit are critical considerations when offering external assistance to schools.

IN THIS EXAMPLE, we again see just how demanding high school reform can be, even when the principal and leadership team are well intentioned, willing participants in school improvement activities. Contextual and related issues such as school size, organizational development, district dynamics, and "fit" with the assistance team, as observed in this vignette, can sidetrack and stall even well-formulated improvement initiatives. Such situations reinforce the importance of constant monitoring of circumstances along the improvement pathway. Organizational agility, flexibility and adjustments are necessary to navigate and overcome barriers to improvement, allowing for the achievement of long-term student and school success.

CHAPTER 7

The Dimensions of Implementation

From Plans to Action

Suzanne M. Stiegelbauer

---

*Suzanne Stiegelbauer was a research consultant for
the School Improvement Network.*

---

*Once there was a very small school that had a very big plan. The school
had collected data on what needed to be improved and had worked
together to make sense of it and figure out what to do about it. The principal took the plan to the superintendent and told her about the changes
she saw for the future and the plans the school committee had developed
to address them. "We have a plan," she said. "Wonderful!" said the
superintendent, "Let's see what happens." A few months later, the superintendent visited the school and asked the principal how her plans were
going. The principal told her about the professional development session
they had and how the teachers and parents were excited about the plan.
"Good," said the superintendent, "I can't wait to see what happens."*

*Near the end of the year the superintendent was visiting the school
again and asked the teachers about the plan and its outcomes. All the
teachers commented on the good ideas in the plan. One said she had
tried some pieces of it; another said that she heard another school had
a plan something like it. "But what difference has it made?" asked the
superintendent, "What has changed?" For many years this continued.
Some things changed; some did not. Some things that were not even
mentioned in the plan changed. Soon a committee developed another
plan. They presented it at a staff meeting for all to hear about. Some
teachers even worked with it. Then the district announced an even
bigger plan.*

THIS SCENARIO is not all that unusual. In the initial excitement about new ideas and their potential, a lot of energy is put into start-up, information sharing, and materials development. And many school leaders believe that if a new idea or program is adopted, after a workshop or two, the desired outcomes will fall in place (Fullan, 2001b; Tobia & Hord, 2002). However, a conversation with any teacher about implementing new programs or procedures is full of tales of false starts, interruptions, no support, and changes in direction just when it gets rolling. Frequently teachers are left on their own to make it work. This assumption of implementation "overlooks the significant work that must occur between the adoption of a program and the realization of its gains" (Tobia & Hord, 2002, p. 2).

In looking at the plans and implementation strategies of the schools involved with Texas State University's School Improvement Network (Gordon, 2006), *high performance schools* were characterized by highly effective implementation of their action research plans. They took steps to provide teachers with time to gather data, reflect, engage in dialogue, plan for continuing improvement, and carry out improvement activities. As one critical friend in the project said, "the main issue that kept coming up from the teachers was time, time, time . . . the school tries to give teachers the gift of time" (p. 10). Gordon describes further:

> High Performance Schools took an incremental approach to implementing their action plans, starting slowly, planning carefully, and developing momentum over time. Professional development was a critical component of each school's action plan, in different formats including study groups, workshops, peer coaching, and ongoing dialogue in small-group and whole-school sessions. Teachers were allowed a great deal of choice regarding which aspects of the action plan they worked on and how they applied the action research in their classroom. It was made clear by administrators and peers that participation was a schoolwide expectation. (p. 11)

Gordon's other categories of schools, *coasters* and *wheel spinners*, did not take as cohesive or internally directive an approach, and experienced much more limited results. His research and the research of his colleagues at Texas State University reinforce the idea that implementation must take into account the multiple *dimensions* of the school environment: the people involved, what the change is, a strategic process for implementation, and supports to keep it going. Some of these dimensions are generic; some are specific to the outcomes and goals that are part of the school's plan. This chapter examines the dimensions of implementation and presents ideas and strategies to help develop an environment in which plans can succeed. However, as Gordon (2006), Fullan (2001b), and others suggest, the implementation of plans may be only the beginning.

A SHORT HISTORY OF IDEAS ABOUT IMPLEMENTATION

One Teacher, One Innovation

Back in the 1970s when the research on change in schools was gathering momentum, change was viewed largely as a classroom issue: one teacher, one classroom, and one innovation. Even into the early 1980s, the thinking on change addressed it as a linear process focusing on a single change in curriculum and instruction (Fullan, 1985). Schools adopted or developed an innovation to meet specific needs with desired outcomes already defined. Some of these adoptions were successful; some were not, in terms of their ultimate success.

For those projects that did not succeed, we now know many of the reasons that influence success for good or bad: lack of match to the environment, lack of follow-through, lack of definition, lack of practice and training in the desired change, and lack of monitoring and evaluation to improve the process. The concept of change as an event brought about by announcing involvement or conducting initial training—and its general lack of success— influenced new research into what happened between adopting a program and getting results. As data from this research began to emerge, it turned out that change was as much, if not more, about the *process*—that part between adoption and results—than about the innovation itself.

Change as Learning

Over the years of research on change, change has come to be viewed differently. Rather than thinking about change affecting one teacher, one classroom, it is now viewed as affecting the very culture of schools. As Larry Cuban (1988) says, many of the early efforts at change might be called "first order changes." They were addressed to more superficial elements of the classroom and school system and did not stress the organization in any meaningful way. However, many of the changes required by current societal and educational demands go deeper than any surface treatment can address, and require what Cuban calls "second order changes"—changes that go deep into the structure of organizations and the ways in which people work together. This kind of change is multifaceted and slower, and requires changing attitudes, perceptions, behaviors, relationships, and the way people collaborate. Plans need to include ways that this multifaceted approach can be tailored to the needs of the environment, both in terms of change-specific implementation strategies and longer term institutional learning.

The old model of change sought to "institutionalize" a change as the end goal of a change process that includes initiation, implementation, and institutionalization—or starting, securing, and sustaining as described by Harris (2002). New models for change see implementation as a learning process that addresses the specific goal of a plan, but goes beyond that to increasing organizational capacity for continuous renewal and growth: "Changing the culture of schools—what schools do and how they work—is the real agenda" (Fullan & Hargreaves, 1992). This has been termed *school renewal* or the *renewing school,* referring to a school that continues to renew and learn from each engagement with change (Hord, 2004). More recent terms such as *professional learning communities* establish this learning process as both a goal and a process. Given that any innovation will likely have a range of effects, many of them changes that occur because of the initial one, the idea of learning and capacity development becomes a necessary part of an organization being "change ready."

Change as Capacity-Building

Planning for change makes the assumption that things will go as planned. In actuality, the multiple dimensions influencing a change process make it less likely to go as planned. Fullan (2001b) uses Patterson, Purkey, and Parker's (1986) concept of change as a nonrational social process that sees the whole system as a series of interacting parts that have potential for change. Change in this context only *begins* with a plan, but must be prepared to be able to work with and learn from whatever comes up in the process. Working with change then becomes a "skill" that can be learned through practice. Developing the knowledge and skills to work with change is a major goal of a learning organization.

Having a plan is a good place to start. The plan organizes the information and provides a sense of direction. Beyond that, it is the capacity of the organization that will make the difference in terms of success. From the initial research on change that approached it as "change-centered" to contemporary approaches that see the multifaceted dimensions of change as a part of learning and capacity development, the key to change is what happens in the process and how it contributes to the growth of an organization that can take on any task.

THE DIMENSIONS OF IMPLEMENTATION

Working with People

To paraphrase the late Matt Miles (1992), and at the risk of overstating the obvious, the secret of change still lies in the applied common sense of the people involved. People know more than they think they know. The problem is putting the knowledge into action—which means reflecting on or processing what they know and developing a flexible sense of where they are going given what they are learning from the process. The baseline for any change is working with the people who will put plans into operation—the people who will lead, support, and act as resources; the people who will act as catalysts and energizers; and the people who will implement and learn.

Anyone who works with schools knows that people are different and will respond to change in different ways. Just like students in the classroom, some will move quickly to learn about the change and some will resist; some will never engage in a meaningful way. The historical role of teachers also shapes their responses. Traditionally, teachers are independent craftspersons who often work in isolation and place great value on the practical outcomes of their work (Huberman, 1983). Teachers' concern about what might be called a practicality ethic means that a change must pass the practicality test—it must be sound, be clear in its goals and procedures, have value to students and outcomes, and be supported by the organization and its leadership. Many teachers feel burned after putting effort into changes that were short-lived, not valued, not clear, not practical for students, and were supplanted overnight by another change.

Fullan (1991, 2001b) asserts that individuals' subjective understanding of the meaning of the change is a strong motivation for commitment to it. Within this "subjective reality," individuals must know enough about a change to decide "what's in it for them" and how they will deal with the new opportunity. It is the "transformation of subjective realities," or the establishment of a new meaning or relationship to the change, that is the essence of a substantive change process (Fullan, 2001b). In the case of being burned by past experiences with change, such negative outcomes reinforce the subjective reality that change is not worthwhile.

Sometimes subjective meaning can be mediated by dealing with the objective reality of the change (i.e., what the change is, how it relates to current practice, what its effects will be, how it fits into the environment). This is Fullan's (2001b) second factor related to meaning. On the one hand is the individual and his or her personal being; on the other hand is the individual's professional life and responsibilities. Somewhere within this framework, change lives or dies for the individual. Research shows that the more contact that occurs within the environment—especially one-to-one and small-group supportive contact (Hall & Hord, 1987, 2001), and group problem-solving or "process analysis" discussions (Miles, 1992)—the more likely that these independent individuals will find meaning in the process and take on the change. Whatever the strategy, it is important that the change be meaningful to teachers. Harris (2002) quotes Gray and Wilcox: "Improvement efforts which duck the question of what's in it for teachers are likely to fail" (p. 41). Anticipating how teachers will respond to the change and even what barriers they might put up goes a long way in facilitating implementation.

Gene Hall, Shirley Hord, Susan Loucks-Horsley, Archie George, and many others involved with the "concerns-based adoption model" or "CBAM" (Hall & Hord, 1987, 2001; Hall & Loucks, 1977) looked at the stages individuals go through when responding to something new. They developed a strategy for support and facilitation based on the developmental sequence found in their research. According to CBAM, individuals progress through concerns related to their personal or subjective experience (self), management and practice with the change (task), and the success of the change on students or others involved (impact). Each of these stages needs to be supported and resolved before the next stage can emerge. Success with implementation occurs when teachers or individuals reach the "consequence" stage, or the stage at which they can see and measure the consequence of the change in terms of positive effects. Facilitators or leaders can use this sequence to design a strategy to support implementation (George, Hall, & Stiegelbauer, 2006).

Because making a change often involves adaptations in behaviors, practices, skills, and even beliefs about what is important and valuable, and potentially challenges what they already do well, people frequently experience initial work with change as a loss of competence (Fullan, 2001b; Marris, 1975). Finding ways to combine their areas of strength with what is new helps promote comfort with change. Although the following sections touch on this in more depth, it is also important to note at this point that how people work together within a change process—their attitude or phi-losophy about it as a collective—can make a difference in the longer term success of implementation and in the organizational capital built through the implementation learning process. Fullan points out that "learning is done best in groups" (Sally Goerner, as quoted in Fullan, 1999, p. 10). Within collaborative cultures, "vitality springs from experiencing conflict and tension in systems which also incorporate anxiety-containing support-ive relationships" (normative structures, roles, working together) (Fullan, 1999, p. 27). As groups work on hard problems, they support each other and are supported by the norms of the institution, as long as the institution does not limit knowledge growth. Group dynamics focused on problem-solving and implementing solutions can help clarify how teachers will approach change, and the dynamics of the group also go a long way toward developing consensus around the value of the change within the organiza-tion (Stiegelbauer, 1996).

Finally, research makes it clear that district, board, and school adminis-trators are the main determinants of whether or not change is implemented. Without their continued and visible support, change has little chance to succeed. However, the role of a leader within a change process, whether as a facilitator of the change or as one who sanctions it, is largely that of "pres-sure and support" (Fullan, 1985; Harris, 2002). Without a certain amount of pressure, nothing happens; without support to tailor change to the needs of individuals and school contexts, not much happens. How leaders do this—and whether the leader is a principal, a district facilitator, a teacher-leader, or a team—depends on the capacity of the organization for "belief in action-in-common" (Donaldson, 2006, p. 105). "This belief, reinforced by shared experience and action, that together the group can accomplish goals that would be difficult to accomplish individually" (p. 105) is the basis for the mobilization of the school to improve.

In considering actions related to implementation based on the issue of *people* facilitators should remember the following:

- Change is a process, not an event. Formulating a plan is an event and potentially the beginning of a process. A process can take many years and have many different areas of emphasis over those years. (The conventional wisdom for implementation, depending on the size of the change, is that it takes three years to produce good outcomes.)
- Individuals respond differently to change; it is a highly personal experience. When change builds on their strengths and offers a

role and capacity to learn based on a shared valuing of the change, individuals are more likely to invest.

- People go through developmental stages related to the self, to management or task, and to the impact or success of the change in terms of outcomes and results. Recognizing these stages will help facilitators develop strategies to support individuals and their implementation. In the *self* stage, people may need information and modeling to see what the innovation is and how it will affect them. In the *task* stage, they need time to practice and ask questions. In the *impact* stage, they need to examine data to see where they are succeeding and to refine what they are doing.

- Teachers are guided by the practicality ethic. They want to know that a change is practical for them to use and will produce beneficial outcomes for them and their students.

- Success in facilitating change requires pressure and support from leaders and facilitators, as well as one-to-one interactions to solve problems and support understanding of the innovation.

- Implementation offers the potential of increasing organizational learning through group interactions as well as individual change, developing the capacity of individuals to lead and of the organization to address ongoing issues.

When outlining a plan for what should happen over a timeline of implementation, these guidelines can act as a foundation for the kinds of actions to be taken over that timeline.

Working with What the Change Is

In planning for change, the attributes of the change itself make a difference to success with implementation. Separate from the people element discussed above, practices or innovations work best when they are classroom- or organization-friendly, well defined, practical, and relevant to real needs. Practices that are too similar or too different from conventional approaches present problems in implementation because teachers either do not clearly distinguish what is new or feel negatively challenged by the size or complexity of a larger scale change.

In adopting already-developed programs, one consideration in addressing teachers' practicality ethic is the "technical rationality" (Miles, 1992) of the programs—that is, ways in which the new programs are expected to be technically better than current practice and to get better results. Programs designed on best practice or those that can show a research base for results require especially close examination in this respect. In the 1980s the emphasis on technical rationality led to an insistence on "innovation quality, fidelity of implementation, and a search for 'teacher-proofness'" (Miles, 1992, p. 9). In the ideal, a technically good innovation should be able to be introduced anywhere with the same results. Later research on change, however, has shown the unlikelihood of such results, even in settings of high competence (Fullan, 1999, 2001b).

The uniqueness of school contexts and environments frequently creates adaptations in "designed from best practice" programs even when there seems to be a good match. Many of these programs prove to be high on cost and low on fit, and to involve "false clarity" (i.e., they appear easy to implement, but actually involve more effort than people anticipate or have been superficially interpreted, as Cuban, 1988, suggests). Huberman (1983), reflecting on the program-based innovations of the 1980s, describes some of the factors affecting implementation and innovation attractiveness, including what he calls *craft legitimization* (i.e., was the product field tested?), *compatibility* (does it fit with the school's ways of doing things?), *accessibility* (is it easily understood by users?), *observability* (can users see its application to their own work, as in descriptions or videos of ideas at work?), *adaptability* (does it contribute to group or organizational learning?), and *inspiration* (are values an important component of its message?). These qualities of innovation reveal a glimmer of the direction research on change would take in the next two decades, with less focus on the innovation and more focus on compatibility, adaptability, and inspiration in tune with the learning organization.

Whether the change is a curriculum program or other classroom-based innovation, whether it affects a specific population or the whole school, there are a few guidelines that can help in the implementation process. The first is *need*. Ideally, change should occur in response to evidence of a need. The term *evidence* is important here, because the definition of the change often relates to what kind of evidence exists. If there is evidence that student discipline is a problem, then that is the focus. If there is evidence that reading needs to be improved, then that becomes the change project. When there is a clear link to need, individuals are more likely to engage with the process. Often changes are introduced because of an educational fad, the interests of new leaders in the district, or even good ideas but not a real need. Action research is one process that helps define what real needs are.

The second guideline involves *clarity*. Clarity refers to a definition of the change in terms of practical expectations for those involved with it. If a change has clarity, people will know what to do, even if doing it involves a learning process. Practical changes are those that address salient needs; fit well in real classroom, teacher, or school situations; are focused; and include concrete how-to-do-it information. One way to improve clarity and reduce the potential for distortion is a method called "innovation mapping" or "innovation configurations" (Hord, Stiegelbauer, Hall, & George, 2006). This method outlines and describes the core features of the change in such a way that users know what to do related to each feature. Change facilitators can use this kind of mapping in professional development, monitoring progress, and assessing outcomes. Mapping may also help determine where the best fit is in terms of the change and the school, adapting some aspects of the change as necessary. This is especially true of already-designed programs. Another part of innovation clarity is the identification of the resources and system supports necessary for the change to proceed as defined.

The third guideline involves *size* and *complexity*. According to several large studies of implementation, the larger the scope of the change and the more personally demanding it is, the greater the chance for success (Crandall, Eiseman, & Seashore Louis, 1986; Fullan, 2001b). Although size and complexity may initially deter potential users, in the longer term the greater the effort expended in implementing a new practice, the greater the potential outcome. Put another way, when the change is seen as valuable and requires new learning that is directed to a valued goal, the effort becomes worthwhile and has an effect on teachers and students. Small innovations often do not succeed because they are not perceived to be worth the effort (not seen as valuable) or because teachers cannot distinguish the innovation clearly enough from other practices. On the other hand, innovations that are too large or that require too much from the organization as a whole frequently result in distortion or partial implementation to make them manageable. In essence, "the greatest success is likely to occur when the size of the change is large enough to require noticeable, sustained effort, but not so massive that typical users find it necessary to adopt a coping strategy that seriously distorts the change" (Crandall et al., 1986, p. 26). The issue of complexity also relates to the process of implementation and will be discussed below. In general, change efforts are always complex but can be made more complex by innovations that have too many pieces.

As an overview, looking at what the change is and how it fits within the organization can be helpful in designing an implementation strategy. Some changes will require more of the organization than others, some will require specialized training, and some will require strategies to engage selected groups such as parents. Understanding what the change is asking people to *do*, and breaking that doing into manageable pieces, can go a long way in moving the change effort forward. The following summary highlights some of the ideas presented about what the change is:

- Any change must fit into the teachers' situations, be clear, and include concrete how-to-do-it information. It must demonstrate clear goals and benefits for students or address other desired outcomes. It must be relevant to local needs and concerns, and be adaptable to local needs and concerns if necessary. Change is not always progress, especially if it does not fit or is imposed without local buy-in.
- Change in practice requires change in behavior, skills, attitudes, beliefs, and, frequently, ways that people work with one another. Each one of these is a kind of innovation in itself and a reason that change is always complex. Change affects not only teachers but also schools and school systems. Changes need to be viewed in relation to other practices and system goals.
- Too small or too large a change may result in no change at all. The greatest success occurs when change requires noticeable, but manageable, and sustained effort.
- Developing a map of the change that shows what is expected in terms of core components, what components may be adaptable, and what needs to be in place related to materials and supports, can help in determining fit and in designing implementation strategies.

Working with Strategies or Processes to Put the Change in Place

Successful change requires a long-term process of action, refinement, and support to clarify and integrate innovation use. Strategies or processes can be considered in terms of three phases: (a) the *initiation* phase, what needs to happen in the early stages of implementation; (b) the *implementation* or "learning and doing" phase, putting the innovation into action and use, with monitoring for refinements; and (c) the *continuation* phase, also called *institutionalization*, where the innovation is working in place and is being assessed to see whether short-term and long-term goals are being met. Evidence suggests that, rather than support institutionalization as an end product, organizations tend to enter a process of *renewal*, which may result in either tailoring the innovation to a more current need or replacing it. Continuation as a term refers more to growth, with the learning gained from implementation at its base. Depending on the nature of the change, going through these phases can take up to three years or more for stable implementation and predictable outcomes.

At any point in this sequence the process may be altered for any number of reasons—change in leadership or goals, for instance—resulting in adaptations to the innovation, partial implementation, or even in dropping it. Fullan has described older approaches to implementation as "hyper-rational," a near lock-step follow-the-directions approach that does not take into consideration the "flow" of organizational life (Fullan, 1991; Wise, 1977). He sees schools as reflecting the "non-rational" or "non-linear" quality of social systems (Patterson et al., 1986). This approach views the whole system as a series of interacting parts that have potential for change. Planning and implementation strategies must have some flexibility in this context and aim for growth and learning as well as specific outcomes. "Have a plan, but learn by doing" (Fullan, 1991, p. 83).

Rather than focusing on a single innovation, many schools now are developing the capacity for continuous improvement as a *generic skill,* based on changing needs and new kinds of programs and professional development structures. Although traditional leadership is important to change and structuring implementation, more frequently *temporary systems*—project groups, task forces, action research teams, consultative relationships, or grade-level groups—are put in place to support the change through implementation, with the expectation that "at some more or less clearly defined point in time [they] will cease to be" (Miles, 1992, p. 9). These temporary groups have the advantage of being able to define themselves, and they are often more egalitarian and experimental than the organizational environment around them. The work of these groups frequently becomes a model for how the school works with change, and "creative attention given to the invention and use of new types of temporary systems could show a very high payoff" (p. 10). As these temporary groups form new norms within the team, they are often able to influence the norms around them to good effect. When the team disbands, members have new skills they can contribute to other projects. In addition, such groups help develop collaborative work cultures that reduce the professional isolation of teachers. As one gains the recognition of one's peers, incentives to succeed increase.

In the never-stopping world of educational change, there have been many handbooks on what kinds of strategies are necessary for implementation of change (Calabrese, 2002; Chenoweth & Everhart, 2002; Fullan, 2001b; Hall & Hord, 1987, 2001; Harris, 2002; among a number of others). In terms of the practical categories of strategies, these handbooks follow much of the same formula. As Hall and Hord (2001) list:

1. Creating a context supportive to change
2. Developing, articulating, and communicating a shared vision of the intended change
3. Planning and providing resources
4. Investing in professional learning
5. Checking on progress
6. Providing continuous assistance (pp. 108–112)

Calabrese (2002) says it even more succinctly:

1. Choose a straightforward, achievable goal
2. Act in proportion to the context and people
3. Sustain action
4. Modify actions to sustain movement (p. 97)

Strategies for implementation refer to what facilitators *do* in the process of putting a change in place. Facilitators can be school leaders, teacher-leaders, committees or teams, or outside consultants. Regardless, any plan for implementation would include strategies such as those listed above, emphasizing recognition of context; the need for real, practical, achievable goals; ongoing support; and evaluation to modify the process for emerging needs. This is a process that could take years and that could experience what Fullan (1991) calls the "implementation dip," where the change seems to be floundering; however, if the change facilitators are persistent, desired outcomes can be achieved. Fullan describes implementation this way:

> Implementation, whether it is voluntary or imposed, is nothing other than a process of learning something new. One foundation of learning is inter-action. Learning by doing, concrete role models, meetings with resource consultants and fellow implementers, practice of the behavior, and the fits and starts of cumulative, ambivalent, gradual self-confidence all constitute a process of coming to see the change more clearly. (p. 85)

Summarizing the major points on actions related to implementation, it is important to think about implementation as being embedded in a system that contains abundant variables. When many of the variables are in support of the change, implementation is more likely to succeed; when conflicting factors intrude, it is less likely to be effective. Social systems are dynamic, and recognizing that fact and working with it, is the best way to approach implementation. Major considerations relating to implementation strategies and processes include the following:

- Implementation may appear to be about one innovation or change, but it is actually embedded in a complex system or beliefs, behaviors, traditions, and other variables. When any change is started, it affects the organization as a whole.
- Organizational themes contributing to successful change include developing a shared vision; evolutionary planning; providing resources; empowering individuals and groups; ongoing professional development; and developing strategies for coping with problems, for analyzing and restructuring organizational norms to support ongoing learning, and for including time to practice with the innovation and observe models of effective use. These themes are interactive and interwoven throughout the process of change.
- Plans may include different strategies for the three phases: (a) initiation, or start-up; (b) implementation, or taking action and engaging in practice with the innovation; and (c) continuation, or measuring effects and keeping the innovation on track. Likewise, plans must include resource development for each of these phases, and for other needs that might arise over an extended period.
- Temporary groups—assigned the creative responsibility for managing change—help develop new relationships and new learning within the organization, as well as more focused activities related to change. If more than one change is being implemented, each might have a temporary group in charge of it and a division of resources.
- The broader agenda of change is the development of an organizational capacity to respond to changing needs and conditions. This capacity can include strategies like action research and professional development. The goal is not mastery of a single innovation but ongoing learning and the development of collaborative work cultures.

Finding Supports for Change as a Learning Process

The most important element of support for change is support for the individuals involved with the change. This support can take the form of coaching, mentoring, peer advising, providing time for practice and discussion, encouragement, facilitating needs, and collecting information about progress and using it—all with the agenda of giving the individuals time and direction throughout the implementation period. Support isn't needed just at the beginning, but must be threaded throughout implementation. In the beginning, teachers need to practically understand what the innovation is.

Through the middle stages, they need support for practice. When their expertise increases, they need support for seeing outcomes (data) and refining their work. Most change processes start with these considerations; few carry them through the whole process.

Second is the issue of resources. When preparing for implementation, the material resources needed for start-up are compiled. Resources, however, also include longer term funding for teacher substitutes, for resupply when materials run out, and for potential consultants or other personnel to help solve problems. Providing resources can also mean finding personnel for special roles. When considering resources, the other levels of the school system come into play—district, system, other schools, other personnel, even the community. Most change is "resource hungry," says Fullan (2001b). District policy decisions about how people relate to each other within and across schools in the district, and how much time is given to working with professional development, can be essential supports for change. Policy can support systemwide initiatives and learning, as well as local projects.

Fullan and Hargreaves (1992) emphasize developing broader system policies that encourage building trust and taking risks, foster interaction and growth, and find ways to empower strong local schools. Such recommendations emphasize the need for systems to develop connectedness and real empowerment—the sharing of power with students, with teachers, and with principals—to tailor their plans to their environment. Rosenholtz (1989), in her research on how schools develop the capacity for change, found that "moving schools" (or improving schools) placed a great deal of emphasis on the selection of good personnel and on learning opportunities for all. Working together builds consensus and a shared belief in the value of the outcomes. Further, working together builds support in the exchange with peers as a professional "learning community" (Gordon et al., 2006; Hord, 2004).

Major points relating to support for implementation include the following:

- People will be more committed to changes that are of local interest to them, whether those changes come from the outside or from the inside. Change as a local initiative should fit within systemwide goals and priorities but still address local needs. Community understanding and support can keep initiatives going.
- The three phases of change—initiation, implementation, and continuation or renewal—each have their own requirements for support. Maintaining a change can be as challenging as initiating

one. Conditions for success remain the same; the presence or lack of supports can make or break change efforts. Implementation should be considered a long-term project.

- The greatest support for change comes from the kinds of learning relationships that can be set up on the inside. An implementation process needs models, teachers, coaches, mentors, and evaluators to address all of its phases. Further, such personnel need to be able to work together positively according to their strengths.
- The focus of policy should be the development of organizational supports and linkages that enable schools to improve. Empowerment means giving people responsibility and support to actualize that responsibility. The presence or absence of supportive policies can determine the success or failure a change effort.
- Districts and schools can improve system capacity for change through selecting good people and providing them with opportunities to learn.
- Change needs to be planned for over an extended period, not just during the early phases. Time, funding, support roles, and supportive policies will all continue to be important throughout the process.

PRACTICAL GUIDELINES FOR IMPLEMENTING PLANS

Implementing new ideas is never without work. The excitement of the beginning soon reveals the need for a plan for the long haul. When the beginning is organized to consider issues such as ongoing support and monitoring, temporary groups as coordinators and facilitators, and policies that make growth easier, positive outcomes are more likely. It is always discouraging to hear about the excitement, and then see that nothing but unfulfilled work came out of it. Further, when new ideas do not take into consideration the people and the context, plans have even less potential of success. Regardless of the current press for better academic outcomes for students, if a system does not have the people and contextual resources, and does not see itself as powerful, change in outcomes becomes more a dream than a reality.

Figures 7.1 through 7.3 provide some guiding questions related to the implementation of change in each of the dimensions discussed in this chapter: people, what the change is, the implementation process, and monitoring and supports. Figure 7.1, *Initiation*, considers the start-up phase of change as the period of defining the work and orienting people and the system to support it. Figure 7.2, *Implementation*, extends those questions to what needs to happen in the task or practice phase, when people and the system learn practically what the change means and how to bring it about. Figure 7.3, *Continuation*, addresses the phase during which the organization examines what has been accomplished, evaluates the process, and makes decisions about how to keep the change going or modify the system further.

Initiation	
DIMENSION	**QUESTIONS TO CONSIDER**
People	• What do teachers know about the change? • What experiences do teachers have that are similar to the change? • What strengths do they bring to the change? • What are the barriers for teachers? • How does the change fit with their values? • What's in it for them? • What are the "self" concerns, and how can they be addressed? • What role do teachers have in the process as individuals, as groups, and as facilitators?
What the innovation is	• Is the change sound and clear? • What does the change ask people to *do*? • How does it relate to current practice? • Is the change classroom/organization friendly? • Does it relate to real needs? • Will it have value to student outcomes? • What does the change look like when in full operation? • Is the change similar to anything already done? • Can the change be approached in stages? • Where would teachers have difficulty? • Why did we decide to implement this change? • Where is the change most likely to be adapted by context? • Where does the change "fit," and what needs to be adapted?

(continued on the next page)

Chenoweth and Everhart (2002) present a similar staged implementation process. From the outset, they advocate developing problem-solving competence, through action research or another inquiry process, to focus on what the problem is and the need for a solution. Like Matt Miles (1992), Chenoweth and Everhart advocate a shared leadership approach,

Initiation *(continued)*	
DIMENSION	**QUESTIONS TO CONSIDER**
Putting change in place	• How does this fit with the mission/culture of the school?
	• How does it fit with the way people work together?
	• In what ways does this create a learning opportunity?
	• What new materials/resources are needed?
	• What materials/resources are available (human resources as well as funding and concrete materials)?
	• What could be anticipated as stumbling blocks?
	• Who can provide leadership?
	• What do teachers need to know to do this?
	• What skills do teachers need?
	• How will we know we are on track?
	• What would be indicators of early success?
Supports	• Does leadership support the change?
	• Is district policy in place to support the change?
	• Who will support? Who will mentor?
	• What will support look like?
	• What are the barriers to support?
	• What kind of evidence do we need to keep support attuned to needs?
	• How can initial and ongoing support be structured?
	• How can we use data to inform support?

FIGURE 7.1

In Figures 7.1 through 7.3, "teacher" is named as the object of change, but change could also be directed to a whole school, an administrative division, or other aspects, depending on what the change is.

Implementation

DIMENSION	QUESTIONS TO CONSIDER
People	• What do teachers need to know about the change? • How are they progressing? • Do they have the information or resources they need? • Do they feel they are part of a whole-school effort? • Do they know where they are in the implementation process? • How many are early adopters who are being successful and can help others? • Are there visible symbols of the change working?
What the innovation is	• Does teacher practice show teachers understand how to *do* the change? • Is the change still within the model as it was designed? • Should the change be approached by components (i.e., not all at once)? • Are there any questions about the change? • Is there something that is not working?
Putting change in place	• Are there data available that reflect the progress of implementation? • What are the indicators of early success, and are any of these indicators present? • What help do teachers need? • Are there data that demonstrate changes in behavior? • Is there evidence of a shared culture with respect to this change? • Are the necessary resources available, including time for practice or coaching? • Are teachers aware of what effects to expect? • Is the team involved in managing the change?
Supports	• Is support still in place to coach teachers? • Have other linkages for support been developed (fellow schools, partnerships, consortia, etc.)? • Are setbacks being handled well? • Do teachers feel they are supported? • How can we use data to inform support?

FIGURE 7.2

Continuation

DIMENSION	QUESTIONS TO CONSIDER
People	• Are teachers aware of successes? • Have teachers been able to report on success and make suggestions for improvement? • Do teachers feel that they are a part of something valuable? • Do teachers have input on the continuation process? • Are teachers able to talk about what they have learned? • Do teachers feel they have made an improvement?
What the innovation is	• Is the change having the desired effects? • Have there been suggestions for further improvements to the change based on data? • Should you be doing something different (renewal)? • How have beliefs and practice changed? • What do we need to adapt about the change?
Putting change in place	• How has the change affected the mission/culture of the school? • How has it changed the way people work together normally? • How has it been a learning opportunity? • Has the change been incorporated into the school ethos? • Who is providing leadership? • How can we maintain vision? • How have outcomes/behavior of students changed? • What data are evidence for positive change? • What data do we still need to collect? • What happens next?
Supports	• How can we overcome change fatigue? • Do we still have support as needed? • How can long-term support be structured? • How can we use data to inform support? • Are teachers aware of outcomes (data)? • Can teachers use outcome data to improve further? • Do participants feel a part of the whole?

FIGURE 7.3

with a temporary group or school team helping to collect and organize data about need and relevance, and perhaps assisting in development of an initial plan. In discussing their "initiation" stage, they talk about "jump starting" the implementation process through helping staff make the transition from what they know to "what can be." This could include such initiation questions as, What experiences do teachers have that are similar to the change? What strengths do they bring to the change? What are the barriers for teachers? How does the change fit with their values? What's in it for them? Chenoweth and Everhart's second stage involves reculturing. This includes creating symbols to show that something is happening—a new culture is developing, change is taking root. Their third or "mature" stage is focused on maintaining the vision through a critical focus on tracking progress.

Using data can be an invaluable part of the change process. In the School Improvement Network, the use of data was stressed as part of assessing and developing action plans. It was stressed again as part of the longer term approach to providing feedback for the implementation and continuance phases. In the successful Network schools, participants were able to develop a group commitment to working with the change and continuing to see it through. This commitment had the additional advantage of strengthening flexibility as complications arose and improvement objectives changed. This flexibility, in turn, provided for capacity development over time, for administrators and teachers alike (Gordon, 2006; Stiegelbauer, Gordon, & McGhee, 2005). As Chenoweth and Everhart (2002) state, "successful schools don't have fewer problems, they just deal with them better" (p. 96); they have developed a capacity for change.

Going back to where we started, "A great majority of policies and innovations over the past 25 years did not get implemented even where implementation was desired" (Fullan, quoted in Baker, 2001, p. 6). This chapter began with an example of good intentions that never went beyond initiation. The real work of change is in the implementation phase. "Success is 25% having the right ideas and 75% establishing effective processes" (Fullan, quoted in Baker, 2001, p. 7). For Fullan and Baker, effective processes are all about relationships. It is relationships that make implementation happen—relationships established through leadership, through making connections with other parts of the system, through support, through trying things out, through being on a team, and through making sense of the change task—that and keeping to the task. The capacity for continuous learning rests on the continuous cultivation of strong working relationships (Baker, 2001).

The successful Network schools continue to be successful through good working relationships and keeping to the task. Being part of a network of peers helped everyone—school administrations and teachers alike—stay on task throughout the action research process.

Considering the various dimensions of implementation offers an opportunity to see how the relationships among people, environments, innovations, and processes can be different in a variety of environments but still the same in principle. It is what happens *between* the start-up and the outcomes that makes the difference.

CHAPTER 8

Action Research to Improve School Culture and Climate

Jane Ross

Jane Ross, a middle school assistant principal, facilitated action research at her own school before becoming a critical friend to a middle school in the School Improvement Network.

FOR MANY school-based educators, the term *external* often carries with it connotations of fiats, mandates, outsiders, power, and distrust. In essence, external "fixes" or external research-based models are viewed as not considering the knowledge of context that can only come from working on, or closely with, a school campus. The idea that research entities—whether people or institutions—beyond schools carry the answers to problems *within* schools can resonate both disempowerment and distrust in the capabilities of the adults and children at the school to identify areas needing improvement and to generate meaningful solutions.

This sense of distrust can produce negative effects on a school's culture and climate. In this chapter, *culture* and *climate* refer to the collective actions, interactions, beliefs, and priorities of an organization (Patton, 2002). Positive school culture and climate can be developed by teachers serving as researchers in collective inquiry designed to resolve problems affecting their unique environment and students. Many schools participating in the School Improvement Network experienced improvements in school climate and culture as a result of engaging in the collaborative action research process. One Network school selected school culture and climate as its specific area of focus, and thus the effects in this area were even greater because both the *process* and the *content* centered on improving school culture and climate. A case study of this school's action research will be shared later in this chapter.

The recursive and reflective nature of action research encourages voice, trust, empowerment, collaboration, and active teacher involvement in school improvement, to name only a few of the tenets of this research method. In contrast to educators working in isolation with often limited involvement in the development of school improvement initiatives, action research sets the stage for the emergence and development of the aforementioned tenets. In action research, teachers are viewed as possessing insight into educational issues affecting their students. Stringer (1999) points out that communication is essential to developing an effective school climate. Action research requires all participants to engage in myriad styles and forms of communication that significantly impact the participants' collective and individual ability to implement and sustain meaningful change.

For a profession in which external mandates, external solutions, and external research dominate, action research provides a welcome relief to instructional leaders who believe that educators, parents, and students at their schools have the intelligence, context knowledge, and resources to examine situational issues and respond to them through in-depth inquiry, evaluation, and action. Miles and Huberman (1994) state, "The analytic tasks [of action research] emphasize the use of action-related constructs, seen in a melioristic frame, and intellectual emancipation through unpacking taken-for-granted views and detecting invisible but oppressive structures"(p. 9). This intellectual relief can serve as a basis for continuous school improvement through the improved culture and climate of a campus. Few educators would disagree that the culture and climate of a campus directly affect the impact and quality of school improvement efforts. Ferrero (2005) argues that "Schools should cultivate a strong sense of community by developing norms for the classroom and school" (Ferrero, 2005, p. 425).

The extent to which interactions among educators are collaborative, professional, and collegial strongly influences the extent to which school culture and climate develop as positive forces on a school campus (Marzano, 2003). Marzano emphasizes the significant effect that a positive school climate has on impacting academic results. As teachers' sense of self-efficacy improves, so do students' sense of self-efficacy (Marzano, 2003).

Often, educational institutions and outside entities advising schools emphasize student academic achievement as the main focus of school improvement efforts. Although this certainly is the ultimate goal of schools, there is an inherent assumption in this advice that the sole way to improve student academic achievement is to focus exclusively on academic achievement. This assumption appears to ignore the fact that there exist myriad influences on individual student and campus-wide academic performance. School culture and climate are two powerful influences on school performance. The environment in which adults and students learn directly impacts student achievement. Action research provides a lens through which an examination and deconstruction of campus culture can occur. This is particularly important, as Eisner (2003) asserts:

> The aims, content, and organization of schools are so embedded in our culture that the assumptions on which they rest are seldom examined . . . the nature of schools is rooted in the historical traditions, values, and assumptions into which we have been socialized. Although we act on these values and assumptions, we seldom examine them. (p. 648)

Stringer (1999) adds, "Traditional approaches to research often involve an adversarial or authoritarian style that reflects the cultural ethos of competition" (p. 20). Conversely, action research promotes a culture of collaboration, trust, engagement, and a spirit of working together to solve problems rather than working in contradiction with one another. According to Schmoker (2004), collaboration among educators improves performance. For an instructional leader who trusts the commitments and capacities of adults and students in schools, individual and collaborative action research takes problem-solving and research to the fine-tuned level that is hard to access without a deep understanding of situational variables, such as school culture and climate. Sarason (1996) eloquently describes the complexity of school change: "The more sensitive you become to . . . complicated embeddedness, the more you realize how many different systems have to change if the change you seek in the schools can be successfully introduced and maintained" (p. 11).

Although many externally generated solutions may incorporate the voices of school-based individuals, the voices rarely appear to be those of the stakeholders within the specific school to which the research is being applied. Often, the result is a decrease in positive school culture and climate as educators feel that research-based initiatives are happening *to* them rather than being developed *with* them. Thus, the change process itself can hinder the very change it is designed to promote. By giving credence to the notion that acculturation within a school setting is significant, action research can more extensively affect positive school improvement.

Action research is such an effective tool for tapping into educator potential and responding to issues through practitioner-centered inquiry that it is difficult to imagine any educator or educational system not gravitating toward it as one tool for improvement. As evidenced by the wide range of action research topics selected by Network schools, the areas of focus in action research are developed organically from those directly affected by a situation; the areas of focus are unique and limitless.

THE INHERENT RELATIONSHIP OF ACTION RESEARCH WITH SCHOOL CULTURE AND CLIMATE

Examining schools often mirrors examining society. Just as societies are comprised of communities reflecting societal culture and climate, so too communities within schools reflect the schools' culture and climate. When school improvement efforts focus only on structural variables, they ignore the political dynamics of the organization (Van den Berg, 2002). Van den Berg argues that a system's patterns of culture, power, and control influence classroom teachers and their instruction. Emotions and cognition go hand in hand. Thus, it would appear logical for a system interested in improving student achievement to focus on improving the culture within the larger environment. Van den Berg further argues that teacher efficacy depends on situational context. Action research focuses on situational context in a way that supports his argument.

Merriam and Simpson (2000) list some of the benefits of action research as being relevant to actual situations, systematic in its process for problem-solving, and responsive to innovation. Action research serves as an effective tool for change through multiple characteristics that promote authentic and sustainable school improvement. Fullan (1999) lists eight lessons toward implementing effective change:

Lesson 1: You can't mandate what matters.
Lesson 2: Change is a journey, not a blueprint.
Lesson 3: Problems are our friends.
Lesson 4: Vision and strategic planning come later.
Lesson 5: Individualism and collectivism must have equal power.
Lesson 6: Neither centralization nor decentralization works.
Lesson 7: Connection with the wider environment is critical for success.
Lesson 8: Every person is a change agent. (p. 18)

These eight lessons, particularly the last one, resonate throughout the action research process.

Action research can provide a safe environment in which teachers experience best practices that can be transferred to the classroom. In essence, teachers who interact as learners have an increased likelihood of establishing and modeling learning partnerships with students and parents (Hargreaves & Fullan, 1998). "Students would be better served if educators embraced learning rather than teaching as the mission of their school" (DuFour, Eaker, & DuFour, 2005, p. 5).

School leaders interested in improving school culture and climate tend to model what they expect through action, verbiage, and priorities (Schlechty, 2002). It is important for school leaders to provide time for collaborative adult learning and opportunities for school educators to examine goals and develop a collective perspective on practice and culture (Darling-Hammond, 2002). The action research cycle provides myriad opportunities for participants to gauge the health of the school community (Calhoun, 1994). Calhoun (1994) notes that in collaborative action research everyone in the school can be involved in the inquiry. Three key goals of collective action research are reducing isolation, contributing to the knowledge base, and gaining voice (Calhoun, 1992). A school principal who promotes these actions moves from being a school manager and instead becomes a "cultural change principal" (Fullan, 2002, p. 17).

School improvement efforts must focus on organizational patterns and variables that connect to adult and student learning. According to Danielson (2002),

> Through a school's organizational patterns . . . the staff can convey to both students and their parents that learning is important, that the business of school is learning, and that the different elements of the school's organization are structured to support that learning. (p. 43)

School culture and climate influence and are influenced by the school's organizational emphasis. Hargreaves and Fullan (1998) argue that long-term exposure to a negative school climate ultimately hurts all stakeholders in multiple ways, particularly in the area of student achievement. Because negative school culture and climate frequently are the results of isolationism and exclusion, the action research form of inquiry increases the likelihood that all stakeholders feel they have something valuable to contribute to school improvement and, ultimately, student achievement.

Collinson and Cook (2007) emphasize the importance of systemic thinking rather than linear thinking to best understand patterns, relationships, and applications. Systemic thinking focuses on interrelationships and how to structure the culture and climate of a school to maximize learning.

EXAMPLES OF ACTION RESEARCH FOR IMPROVED SCHOOL CULTURE AND CLIMATE

Here I will describe three examples of action research to improve school culture and climate: two at a middle school where I serve as assistant principal for curriculum and instruction, and the third at a middle school in a different school district that was a member of the School Improvement Network. I served as the critical friend for the Network school.

Action Research for Teacher Retention

Without a sense of schoolwide continuity, the emergence of a positive school culture and climate is difficult. When faculty constantly changes through attrition, the sense of schoolwide community is at risk. Part of developing and sustaining a positive school culture and climate is through an ancestry of personnel. With this notion in mind, a group of teachers at a middle school campus engaged in action research centered on reducing the teacher attrition rate. We analyzed historical demographic data about teachers who left and developed a profile of a teacher with a higher than average likelihood of leaving the profession.

Our interview data included exit interviews with teachers who had decided to leave the school, as well as interviews with those teachers who were in the process of deciding whether they were going to leave. We learned that school culture and climate directly impacted the individual's decision about remaining, particularly on a high-needs campus. We found that one reason teachers resigned was a sense of isolation. Calhoun (1992) argues that as long as educators solve problems in isolation, classroom excellence is difficult to achieve, and frustration results. This frustration makes the work environment intellectually and emotionally uninviting for teachers. Barth (2006) expands on this idea:

> Empowerment, recognition, satisfaction, and success in our work—while in scarce supply within our schools—will never stem from going at it alone as a masterful teacher, principal, or student, no matter how accomplished one is. Empowerment, recognition, satisfaction, and success come only from being an active participant within a masterful group—a group of colleagues. (p. 13)

Many of the teachers whom we interviewed decided to stay, and indicated that part of their decision included the fact that we had listened to their voices during the action research process. An institution that honors individual and collective voice tends to set the stage for the emergence of a positive school climate. Strategies that provided additional support for struggling teachers were selected and implemented by teams of teachers working with those who were feeling burned out. These strategies included peer coaching, mentoring, study groups, and paperwork support sessions, to name only a few. Such activities promote collaboration and reflection, which in turn promote a sense of community, belonging, and ownership.

The recursive process of planning, action, evaluation, and modification within action research ensured that the assistance provided was responsive to the ever-changing context at our school. Schools are complex entities that experience ongoing change. External research often examines problems through a fixed lens that may not apply to all campuses. Even when traditional research matches the needs of a campus, it is impossible for the research to consider, or even know, all of the variables that influence that campus's improvement continuum and needs. By reducing the teacher attrition rate on our campus, teacher inquiry had an increased likelihood of being sustained. As with most action research endeavors, additional school improvement benefits emerged from the main focus of reducing teacher attrition to further improve school culture and climate. In this case, student achievement increased and student discipline issues decreased.

Action Research to Improve Student Writing

Climate and culture must be nurtured at the classroom as well as the school level. We also used action research to improve both classroom climate and student writing on our campus. Before this action research effort, teachers taught writing with limited student input on the actual process. Classrooms were characterized by teacher-led instruction rather than student-centered learning within an environment of trust and input.

Data sources included interviews with students and teachers centered on understanding the elements of effective writing, as well as the things that influence a student's desire to write and the quality with which the writing is performed. By including student input at the beginning of writing assignments, students were able to help determine the elements of effective writing through criteria charts and then develop rubrics to measure various gradations of success with each criterion.

This action research centered on students learning elements of effective writing through student-led goal-setting. As Perchemlides and Coutant (2004) note, when students are presented with the opportunity to examine and evaluate their own writing, they are able to identify their areas of growth. This act fosters an empowering and efficacious climate and culture in the class. Through focusing on the climate of the classroom rather than only focusing on the logistics of writing, students' sense of empowerment increased. When students' sense of empowerment and self-efficacy increased, improved writing emerged.

Our research incorporated the input of students and teachers, whose evolving experiences were interwoven throughout the action steps and program evaluation. Results once again transcended the specified focus areas and people directly involved, and positively affected the entire school. By improving students' writing on our campus, all subject areas benefited. Student and teacher efficacy improved, and a sense of community emerged through a schoolwide focus on writing. Thus, action research went beyond the logistics of academic improvement into the realm of the culture and climate that affect academic improvement.

Collaborative Action Research to Improve School Culture and Climate

The preceding two examples were cases in which educational peers and I engaged in action research on the campus at which we worked; in a third action research initiative, through the School Improvement Network I facilitated action research on a different campus from the perspective of a critical friend. This experience provided a unique vantage point through which my understanding of action research broadened. Although school-based inquiry centers on situated context, the contributing human and research resources are not necessarily exclusively internal. In fact, action research, which honors both internal and external perspectives, works in harmony by considering both subjective and objective views of the area of focus. I served as the Network's critical friend to Centerpoint Middle School as they experienced schoolwide action research for the first time.

During spring 2003, the faculty at Centerpoint engaged in collaborative inquiry to determine possible areas for campus-wide school improvement. I met with the principal, a passionate and dedicated educator, and her action research leadership team as they worked through the process of selecting a focus area. They graciously welcomed me as a critical friend to their team and, together, we brainstormed ideas about their focus area and how to authentically engage the entire school. As an educator who has spent her entire career on a middle school campus, I was able to understand the middle school context around which their discussions evolved. From the beginning of my relationship with the school, there appeared to be a two-way positive connection, which was cultivated at the initial Network meetings with all participating schools. After extensive discussion and reflection, the campus reached consensus that improving school culture and climate would be the focus area. Through further faculty input—including surveys, focus meetings, climate inventories, and a review of archival data—three objectives emerged within the larger focus area: improving safety, improving productivity, and improving collegiality. These three areas directly affected all aspects of school life.

For the purpose of planning, organizing, and evaluating, the faculty developed qualitative and quantitative data collection tools and analysis processes. As the critical friend throughout their action research journey, I assisted the school by reviewing feedback forms; attending faculty and teacher-leader meetings; co-facilitating professional development; collecting and analyzing data from faculty, parents, and students; reviewing progress; and providing ongoing feedback. In addition to on-site visits, we met throughout the year at Network meetings hosted by Texas State University, meetings during which we reflected on progress and challenges as we developed our next steps. The regular meetings with the Network further evidenced that action research does not discount outside support; rather, it uses external resources and perspectives while engaging campus-based practitioners toward self-empowerment.

From the outset, I felt honored to serve as Centerpoint's critical friend. The dedication that I observed among the school's teachers and staff was inspiring. As the critical friend, I worked collaboratively with university professors and school faculty in developing data collection and analysis processes. I viewed my role of critical friend as being a flexible one, and I was ready and eager to adapt in response to the campus's needs within the larger framework of action research.

Some of my key roles were to assist the school in developing, organizing, reorganizing, and evaluating their activities within a recursive model. The principal, an exceptional instructional leader, provided time, resources, and support as the research unfolded. Her leadership set the tone of risk-taking, trust, empowerment, and innovation that helped form the foundation of the action research. I realized as we continuously reviewed the school's progress that the team often was unaware of the high quality of their implementation strategies. Whenever we met, they expressed their amazement at realizing how much they were accomplishing and at the already emerging positive effects. Too often, instructional leaders become so focused on the multifaceted day-to-day operations that they do not notice the direct and indirect implementation and effects of their hard work. One of my roles was to encourage the team to find time to reflect on their research. It was motivating to watch everyone finally "pat themselves on the back" with pride when they took the time for deep individual and collaborative reflection.

We kept our documentation organized and updated to provide clear evidence of the school's progress toward improving safety, productivity, and collegiality. Although some of the strategies and activities evolved over the course of the year, the overarching focus on improving the school's culture and climate did not change. The faculty viewed the action research as a long-term journey that would span many years.

We reached consensus on our key successes and challenges and celebrated the "living" research. The main successes revolved around the cyclical process of problem-identification, individual and collaborative planning, organization for action, multidimensional improvement activities, and data-based evaluation. The result was a dramatically improved school culture and climate.

As a collaborative team, we agreed that the part of the process that required future improvement was the evaluation component. Although frequent and varied evaluation occurred, it was used primarily to examine and understand effects rather than as a tool for developing modifications in the action plan. By the end of my work with the school, deep mutual respect and admiration had developed among everyone involved, and we all expressed our hope for continuing our communication beyond the end of our formal relationship. The learning and benefits of the relationship were reciprocal and were based on tapping into multiple perspectives to create something good for students. When a person experiences the honor that I had of meeting and connecting with such a dynamic team of educators, the bond is permanent.

Alma Harris (2002) believes that there should exist a combination of pressure and support for school improvement. I was there to provide this balance of support and pressure by assisting educators with the action plan and keeping them focused. Instructional leaders who use action research as a tool for engagement, inquiry, and professionalism increase the likelihood that school improvement will be substantive and sustained. In all of my experiences with action research, it has meaningfully tapped into multiple perspectives and school-based capacities, experiences, innovations, scholarship, and commitments to create something wonderful for students and their academic achievement.

FINAL THOUGHTS ON THE RELATIONSHIP OF ACTION RESEARCH WITH IMPROVING SCHOOL CULTURE AND CLIMATE

Action research underscores collaboration and communication among school-based educators through critical examination of context-specific problems and solutions. The collaborative process in and of itself contributes to a more positive school climate that both transcends and permeates the classroom environment. When teachers' voices are heard and valued as part of their authentic participation in the school improvement process, they feel empowered. Empowerment can result in educators who are willing to initiate and support increasingly ambitious school improvement efforts.

Action research reduces the sense that change in practice is forced upon educators; rather, they organically determine what specific practices need to occur in order for student achievement to increase. The likelihood of efforts being sustained depends on the level of ownership by teachers. DuFour (2004) notes that ownership is achieved through a "culture of collaboration" (p. 9) in which educators recognize that they must work together to promote this type of school climate.

Teachers who engage in schoolwide action research possess a model of recursive reflection that can also be used in the classroom. Thus, students become direct benefactors of their teachers' learning through empowerment, voice, and engagement. When teachers teach the way they learn, and the learning process is meaningful, then students are provided with an environment in which they develop their own voice and ways to influence change. Schlechty (2002) states, "The level and type of engagement affect directly the effort that students expend on school-related tasks" (p. xvii). The likelihood of meaningful engagement within classrooms increases as teachers experience meaningful engagement within schools.

Because action research tends to focus on context-specific goals designed to benefit students, teachers are able to see a direct connection between their efforts and the effects on student learning. Calhoun (1994) points out that schools as centers of inquiry become self-renewing entities. The act of engaging in action research increases organizational efficacy. The culture and climate of a campus can improve dramatically when stakeholders see a direct connection between effort and results. When a campus's action research is centered specifically on improving the culture and climate of the campus, then the impact on culture and climate is magnified. Rust and Freidus (2001) provide an eloquent summary of the impact of school culture on school improvement:

In the current press for immediate achievement gains, change agents find themselves teaching technical skills to enhance the quality of teachers' repertoires. This is understandable and laudable. But given what is known about the culture of schools, the isolation that most teachers experience in their schools, the importance of encouragement and support from colleagues and leaders, and the necessity for time to study and reflect on their work, it is vitally important to understand that cultural change must be part of any change that is expected to last. (p. 159)

The recursive and reflective nature of the action research process sets the stage for improved schoolwide culture and climate by fostering authentic voice, focused engagement, contextual understanding, and educator-developed change. The combination of these elements promotes improvement in school culture and climate, and ultimately in student achievement.

CHAPTER 9

In the Beginning

Action Research in a New School

Barbara Davis and Iris Escandón

Barbara Davis was a critical friend for the School Improvement Network, and Iris Escandón was a teacher-leader at one of the Network schools.

CONDUCTING SCHOOLWIDE ACTION RESEARCH at a new campus could be characterized as the best of times and the worst of times—the best because a newly assembled faculty can create a culture of inquiry from the very beginning of the school's existence, and the worst because of the innumerable tasks involved in opening a new school. This chapter describes how the faculty at a new campus dealt with the demands of opening a new school and still managed to implement action research during their first year together.

Gonzales Elementary School opened its doors for approximately 700 pre-kindergarten through fifth-grade students and 45 faculty members in August 2003. Gonzales is located in one of the fastest growing districts in Texas, one that stretches along both sides of an interstate highway in a densely populated area.

An ethnically diverse campus, the Gonzales population includes 5% African American, 64% Hispanic, 30% White, and 1% Other ethnic groups. Approximately 58% of the students are economically disadvantaged, and 27% are English Language Learners.

Named for a long-time advocate for education in the local community, the school's vision reflects its namesake's dedication to education: "Gonzales Elementary School is dedicated to developing a family of life-long learners who view education as the key to the future." The school's principal elaborated on the vision:

> *Every person at Gonzales will be a life-long learner, including the students, parents, and teaching staff. Children will be given opportunities*

to think critically, raise high-level questions, and become self-reliant, productive citizens. . . . Teachers will be empowered to research new strategies and ideas that meet the needs of the diverse group of learners in their classrooms.

The school maintains a strong multicultural environment and features a dual-language program. Using a 50/50 immersion model, English-speaking and Spanish-speaking students receive content instruction in both languages within the same classroom. For social interactions, teachers alternate between English and Spanish, whereas all students receive literacy instruction in their native language. This innovative model began with 44 kindergarten students and progresses through the grade levels as the students are promoted.

GETTING STARTED

Based on her vision of empowering students, teachers, and parents, the principal welcomed the opportunity to collaborate with the School Improvement Network on an action research project. Prior to the school's opening, the principal invited four newly hired teachers to serve as members of a leadership team which, along with her, would meet regularly with the Network. The leadership team included two second-grade teachers (one of whom was Iris, the second author of this chapter), a fifth-grade teacher, and the campus technologist. Barbara (the first author of this chapter) joined the leadership team as the Network critical friend during the fall semester. In this role, she attended Network workshops with the team, made site visits to the campus, and assisted in the planning and evaluation process. As a university faculty member, Barbara also taught undergraduate field-based reading courses at Gonzales two days per week. Therefore, she had numerous opportunities to establish relationships with the teachers and administrators.

The teachers on the leadership team shared responsibility for coordinating three groups of teachers, known as *cadres*. The purpose of the cadres was to build a community of learners within the whole school. Meeting monthly, each cadre focused on a different area, including (a) Community, (b) Student, and (c) Faculty/Staff. All faculty members selected a cadre in which to participate.

Another responsibility of the leadership team was to identify a focus area for action research. Because all of the students, parents, and teachers would be coming together to form a new campus, the team originally discussed the need to focus on building community and morale at Gonzales. However, after examining the spring state assessments of incoming students, the principal recognized a need to address student reading achievement. For example, she found that only 71% of the future Gonzales fourth- and fifth-graders had met the minimum requirements on the reading portion of the Texas Assessment of Knowledge and Skills (TAKS) during the previous year's test administration. She brought this finding to the attention of the leadership team. Based on this and other preliminary data, the team tentatively decided to address both reading achievement and community-building in the action research project.

To involve more members of the faculty in the decision-making process, the leadership team met with Gonzales teachers during the summer months before the school opened. As a new faculty, they discussed plans for the coming year. Frequently, the need for both a cohesive literacy program and community-building dominated the discussions. Because most of the faculty had received district training in guided reading, many expressed a desire for help in implementing this instructional strategy in their classrooms.

The leadership team, with the assistance of the School Improvement Network, discussed ways to combine the need for community-building with the concern for students' reading achievement. Peer coaching, a collaborative method of professional development, seemed to provide an answer.

Once the school year began, the leadership team shared the purpose of the action research project during a faculty meeting. To further validate the need to address reading achievement, members of the Faculty/Staff Cadre collected additional data by informally asking a random sample of teachers to share their most pressing classroom concerns. Teacher comments such as "Not all the kids know their letters and sounds," "They [students] have a difficult time with writing," and "They [students] don't understand what they are reading" confirmed the need to address literacy skills as part of the action research project. Teachers were also asked what they knew about peer coaching. Most of the teachers in the sample indicated they had some knowledge of the process.

The focus for the Gonzales action research became "Improve the implementation of guided reading through the use of peer coaching in order to increase student reading achievement."

TARGET DATA

Both quantitative and qualitative data were collected during the action research project. The Student Cadre collected pre- and post-test data on student reading performance from the classroom teachers. The Faculty/Staff Cadre gathered information on teachers' perceptions of the peer coaching and guided reading processes.

Scores on the Developmental Reading Assessment (DRA) (Beaver, 2001) were used to measure first- and second-grade reading performance. The Quick Phonics Screener (QPS) (Hasbrouck & Parker, 2001) was administered in first through fifth grades to assess word analysis skills. Fall premeasures on all of the reading assessment instruments (DRA, QPS, and district benchmarks based on the state achievement test) demonstrated that Gonzales students performed more poorly than did students on other elementary campuses in the district. This finding underscored the need to focus on reading achievement.

To determine teachers' confidence levels in implementing guided reading and peer coaching, the leadership team developed a 23-item self-assessment survey (see Figure 9.1).

The team adapted the guided reading portion of the survey from a matrix developed by district reading facilitators. Two doctoral students associated with the Network reviewed the instrument. Based on their recommendations and the results of a field test with a small group of teachers, the team administered the revised survey to faculty during an after-school meeting in the fall semester. Teachers rated themselves on various items using a 4-point continuum that ranged from weak (1 point) to strong (4 points). Thirteen items focused on the implementation of guided reading in the classroom (e.g., organizing for guided reading, using materials, and developing resources). The remaining 10 items focused on the teachers' perceptions of personal challenges related to peer coaching.

ACTION PLAN OBJECTIVES

Once the preliminary data were analyzed, the leadership team began developing an action plan. The objectives of the plan included the following:

* Teachers will become more self-aware of their teaching practices
* Teachers will feel confident sharing successes and concerns
* Teachers will implement best practices in literacy instruction through peer coaching
* Students' reading scores on state and district assessments will increase

THE PEER-COACHING PROGRAM

The leadership team felt it was important to train the whole faculty in peer coaching so that everyone would be better prepared to begin coaching during the spring semester. With the help of two graduate students who

Self-Assessment Survey: Guided Reading

Directions: Please indicate your confidence level for each of the following issues involving the Guided Reading process.

Topic	Self-Evaluation			
	Weak			Strong
ORGANIZATION				
Organizing the classroom (physical grouping, centers, etc.)	1	2	3	4
Organizing students into groups (levels, needs, interests, etc.)	1	2	3	4
Organizing students in general (centers, skills practice, etc.)	1	2	3	4
Organizing self (data, books/materials, activities, etc.)	1	2	3	4
Scheduling (time of day, length of groups, etc.)	1	2	3	4
MATERIALS				
Matching students' needs to books	1	2	3	4
Choosing pertinent activities and practice (paper & non-paper)	1	2	3	4
Using teaching supports effectively (white board, sticky notes, etc.)	1	2	3	4
Paperwork maintenance: teacher (anecdotal, check sheets, etc.)	1	2	3	4
Paperwork maintenance: student (reader's notebook, journals, etc.)	1	2	3	4

(continued on the next page)

Self-Assessment Survey: Guided Reading *(continued)*

Topic	Self-Evaluation			
	Weak			Strong
RESOURCES				
Making use of available resources (books, articles, websites, etc.)	1	2	3	4
Development of resources (ideas, experiences, etc.)	1	2	3	4
Developing ideas with others (brainstorming, etc.)	1	2	3	4
PERSONAL CHALLENGES RELATED TO PEER COACHING				
Being assessed by strangers	1	2	3	4
Requesting assistance	1	2	3	4
Dealing with lack of assistance	1	2	3	4
Incorporating new ideas	1	2	3	4
Sharing your ideas with others	1	2	3	4
Being an active, responsive listener	1	2	3	4
Being videotaped	1	2	3	4
Being mentored	1	2	3	4
Mentoring others	1	2	3	4
Being involved in peer coaching	1	2	3	4

FIGURE 9.1

participated in the Network as part of their coursework, the team developed a peer-coaching training session. In February, the team and graduate students presented the training to the faculty. The presenters emphasized the non-evaluative and collaborative nature of peer coaching (Diaz-Maggioli, 2004; Galbraith & Anstrom, 1995; Glickman, 2002; Robbins, 1991). They adopted the "study team" approach to peer coaching. In this model, pairs of teachers work together to support one another's teaching practices and study the impact on student performance (Southeast Comprehensive Assistance Center, 2004). Also referred to as "collaborative coaching" (Diaz-Maggioli, 2004) and "reciprocal peer coaching" (Gordon, Butters, Maxey & Ciccarelli, 2002), this model allows participants to share power equally. Together "they build shared knowledge that is directly relevant to their work" (Diaz-Maggioli, 2004, p. 79).

During the training session, each faculty member listed three other teachers with whom he or she would be willing to partner in the coaching process. All of the teachers on the faculty, including those in special areas (e.g., library, music, art, and technology), were required to participate in peer coaching. Based on the teachers' preferences, the Faculty/Staff Cadre formed peer-coaching teams. These teams, known as PALS (Performance and Learning Supporters), were encouraged to conduct three peer-coaching sessions during the spring semester.

Teacher pairs typically began each peer-coaching cycle with an informal discussion about what they would like their partner to observe during guided reading. PALS determined the day and time of the visit and the post-conference. They also decided on data collection methods.

In addition to training and pairing teachers, the leadership team developed plans for scheduling and monitoring progress. Throughout the peer-coaching process, members of the leadership team served as facilitators who provided assistance to teachers as needed. In addition, Iris created a brochure (see Figure 9.2) that highlighted important components of peer coaching. The brochure served as a reference tool for teachers to use throughout the project.

The leadership team also placed a peer-coaching binder in the teachers' workroom. This notebook included examples of observation instruments, a time frame for completing the peer-coaching cycles, and other pertinent materials.

EVALUATING YEAR 1 OF THE ACTION RESEARCH

At the end of the first year of action research, teachers completed the same self-assessment instrument that they had completed the fall before, to determine what influence peer coaching had had on their development in using guided reading. Additionally, the leadership team developed an end-of-year reflection survey that sought to determine teachers' perceptions of the peer-coaching process. The seven-item survey (Figure 9.3) contained both closed- and open-ended questions. The QPS, DRA, and state achievement test in reading were administered as post-measures of student achievement. Below we review findings from the analysis of student and teacher data.

Student Reading Achievement

Results of the first- through fifth-grade reading assessments indicated that the students had improved in both word analysis and comprehension skills. For example, a comparison of the pre- and post-test scores for first through fifth grades on the QPS (Hasbrouck & Parker, 2001) indicated that student skills in word analysis had improved on all 11 tasks administered to first- through fifth-graders. As shown in Table 9.1, scores on the post-test DRA (Beaver, 2001) demonstrated that a greater percentage of first- and second-graders were reading on or above level in the spring than in the fall semester. In addition, third- through fifth-grade reading scores on the spring admin- istration of the state test (TAKS) improved across all three grade levels, as shown in Table 9.2.

TABLE 9.1   DRA Reading Level Percentages for First- and Second-Graders

Grade	Below Level		On or Above Level	
	Fall	Spring	Fall	Spring
1st	61%	33%	38%	67%
2nd	34%	21%	66%	79%

TABLE 9.2   Percentage of Third- Through Fifth-Graders Meeting Minimum Requirements in Reading

Grade	District Benchmarks		TAKS
	November	January	April
3rd	59%	74%	89%
4th	63%	56%	69%
5th	72%	73%	78%

Survival
Guide
To
Peer Coaching

By Iris Escandón

Principles of Peer Coaching

- Not an evaluation
- Based on TRUST
- All teachers have expertise to contribute
- Helps teachers become more self-directed
- Collegial relationship
- NonJUDGEmental
- Data driven
- Flexible
- Ongoing

Scheduling

1. Meet with PALS at least three times, following peer coaching model:
   a. Pre-conference
   b. Observation
   c. Analysis
   d. Post-conference
   e. Reflection
2. Turn in documentation:
   a. Notes from pre- and post-conferences
   b. Reflective journal questions
   c. Student/class data (DRA, QPS, etc.)
   d. Final survey (to be done in April)
   e. Final summative interview with administrators

Steps of Peer Coaching

Pre-Conference

1. Start positive
2. Teacher shares concerns
3. Choose lesson to be observed
   a. Objectives
   b. Instructional strategies
4. Decide on data collection method
5. Logistics (how, where, what)
6. Set post-conference location/time
7. Review decisions
8. End on positive note

Observation Strategies

Verbatim
Open narrative
Classroom diagramming
Levels of questioning
Videotape
"Homemade" and other

Analysis and Strategy

Coach reviews the teacher's original request, reviews his/her observation notes, and summarizes or categorizes as necessary. Do not include any evaluative statements.

Post-Conference

1. Start on positive note
2. Observer shares/explains data
3. Discussion of data by both participants
4. Create improvement plan
5. Follow-up plan (observer asks what else can be done to further assist)
6. Review post-conference decisions
7. End on positive note

Individual Reflection

Put thoughts/plans on paper:
- Did peer coaching help improve literacy instruction?
- Suggestions for improving the process

DO:
- Listen actively
- Pause ... and make reflective statements
- Insert neutral probing questions
- Bite your tongue!
- Let the peer fill silent gaps
- Review only written data
- Leave other concerns for future visits

DON'T:
- Blame, praise, or judge
- Set yourself as an example
- Offer solutions on your own
- Examine other concerns

FIGURE 9.2 Peer Coaching Brochure

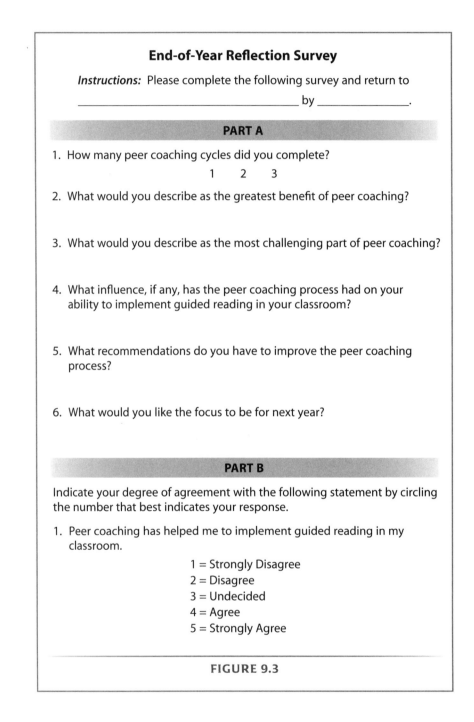

End-of-Year Reflection Survey

Instructions: Please complete the following survey and return to

_____ by _____.

PART A

1. How many peer coaching cycles did you complete?

    1   2   3

2. What would you describe as the greatest benefit of peer coaching?

3. What would you describe as the most challenging part of peer coaching?

4. What influence, if any, has the peer coaching process had on your ability to implement guided reading in your classroom?

5. What recommendations do you have to improve the peer coaching process?

6. What would you like the focus to be for next year?

PART B

Indicate your degree of agreement with the following statement by circling the number that best indicates your response.

1. Peer coaching has helped me to implement guided reading in my classroom.

    1 = Strongly Disagree
    2 = Disagree
    3 = Undecided
    4 = Agree
    5 = Strongly Agree

FIGURE 9.3

Teacher Learning Outcomes

Findings from the pre- and post-school-year self-assessment surveys and the end-of-year reflection survey suggest that peer coaching had a positive influence on the implementation of guided reading. As Table 9.3 demonstrates, teachers' confidence in their ability to use guided reading increased in all areas. The greatest gains occurred in the teachers' ability to organize students for guided reading and in their use of teaching materials. Regarding personal challenges related to peer coaching, the teachers developed the most in their ability to incorporate new ideas and to be mentored by other teachers.

Reflection survey results revealed that all of the respondents had participated in peer coaching. Fifty-six percent participated in three or more peer-coaching cycles, and the remaining 44% participated in two cycles. Regarding the perceived value of the sessions, 50% of the teachers agreed or strongly agreed that peer coaching had helped them implement guided reading, 12% disagreed or strongly disagreed, 20% were undecided, and 18% did not respond to the item.

Responses to open-ended survey questions provided more in-depth information related to the teachers' perceptions of the action research project. Responses were organized into the following categories: (a) benefits, (b) challenges, (c) recommendations, and (d) next steps. Question-by-question responses are discussed below.

Benefits. In response to the question, "What would you describe as the greatest benefit of peer coaching?" several themes emerged. First, respondents reported that they gained knowledge in classroom management and teaching strategies. One teacher noted, "As an observer, you notice some aspects you do not as you teach. [I] learned other strategies especially in managing student behavior." Others commented on the benefit of being able to discuss problems in the classroom, getting input on guided reading strategies, and receiving assistance with organizing materials.

Receiving feedback from their peers was another perceived value of peer coaching. Respondents commented on how helpful it was to have a teacher from another grade level observe and provide comments and suggestions. Others valued the constructive feedback, useful ideas, and suggestions from another person. A novice teacher wrote, "As a first-year teacher, it was beneficial for me to observe teachers in their rooms. It was also helpful to get feedback on my teaching."

The responses also revealed that some participants had become more reflective in their teaching. For instance, one teacher noted, "It called my

TABLE 9.3 Guided Reading Self-Assessment Survey Results at the Beginning and End of the School Year

	Pre-Year Rating ($N = 29$)	Post-Year Rating ($N = 30$)	Increase in Rating
ORGANIZATION			
Organizing the classroom	3.00	3.60	0.60
Organizing students into groups	2.92	3.62	0.70
Organizing students in general	2.70	3.70	1.00
Organizing self	2.75	3.30	0.55
Scheduling	2.64	3.73	1.09
MATERIALS			
Matching students' needs to books	2.54	3.45	0.91
Choosing pertinent activities and practice	2.54	3.38	0.84
Using teaching supports effectively	2.71	3.69	0.98
Paperwork maintenance: teacher	2.39	3.23	0.84
Paperwork maintenance: student	2.39	3.40	1.01
RESOURCES			
Making use of available resources	2.68	3.33	0.65
Development of resources	2.82	3.40	0.58
Developing ideas with others	3.11	3.47	0.36
PERSONAL CHALLENGES			
Being assessed by strangers	2.54	3.40	0.86
Requesting assistance	2.93	3.53	0.60
Dealing with lack of assistance	2.44	3.25	0.81
Incorporating new ideas	3.00	3.90	0.90
Sharing your ideas with others	3.18	3.83	0.65
Being an active, responsive listener	3.36	3.87	0.51
Being videotaped	2.37	2.97	0.60
Being mentored	2.50	3.43	0.93
Mentoring others	2.71	3.52	0.81
Being involved in peer coaching	2.61	3.46	0.85

Teachers rated themselves on a 4-point continuum that ranged from weak (1 point) to strong (4 points). Ratings reported are means of the responses.

attention to areas of my teaching that I may never have realized." Another stated, "The greatest benefit was being able to reflect on specific information from the observation—great insight."

Challenges. According to the survey, time was the most challenging aspect of peer coaching. Of the 34 respondents, 26 (76%) commented on the difficulty in finding time to meet with other teachers. Representative comments include the following: "Finding time to go do observations! Because we were on different grade levels it was hard to find time to meet." "Finding time to meet with my partner." and "Fitting the three cycles in the given time frame." Of lesser concern were issues related to giving constructive feedback and being observed by others.

Influence on ability to implement guided reading. In response to the question, "What influence, if any, has the peer coaching process had on our ability to implement guided reading in your classroom?" the majority of teachers (62%) commented that it had a positive influence. Examples of positive responses included "[I] gained more confidence and [was] given strategies to use for classroom management." [I have a] clearer idea of what is involved in guided reading. . . . Also, I have a better picture of the pace needed." and "It helped improve my questioning strategies."

Not all of the respondents perceived peer coaching to be a valuable experience. Seven teachers indicated the process had not influenced their implementation of guided reading, and six participants did not respond to the item.

Recommendations. Logistical issues and the relevancy of the focus area emerged as themes from the teachers' recommendations. Suggestions for better logistics included starting peer coaching earlier in the year and providing time to work with PALS during faculty meetings. The second major theme of the recommendations focused on having the process be more relevant to individual teacher's needs. Several faculty members suggested that teachers be allowed to select a focus area based on the needs in their own classrooms rather than having a single focus for the entire school.

Next steps. The final open-ended question on the reflection survey asked teachers what they would like to focus on during the next school year. Although reading instruction remained the most frequently occurring response (43%), math instruction was second (23%), and various other areas were mentioned (e.g., community-building, classroom management, science, etc.).

DRAWING CONCLUSIONS FROM
OUR FIRST-YEAR EXPERIENCE

Ultimately, the goal of the action research was to impact student reading achievement by improving teaching practices. The Gonzales faculty, in collaboration with the School Improvement Network, took a proactive stance in achieving this goal. As the results of the data analysis suggest, the project had a positive influence on student learning and teacher professional development.

At the beginning of the year, conducting a schoolwide action research project at a new school seemed like an overwhelming task. However, with the assistance of the School Improvement Network, the project became doable. Working together toward a common goal helped the faculty develop a greater sense of collegiality and oneness. Teachers frequently cited "learning from others" as one of the benefits of peer coaching.

The teachers found, as Calhoun (2004) points out, that action research increased individual expertise and at the same time built a strong professional community. Observing in another teacher's classroom and discussing problems related to instructional practices helped alleviate the sense of isolation that many teachers experience. In addition, conducting schoolwide action research from the beginning of the school's existence established a culture of inquiry that has become the norm for the Gonzales faculty.

Although the first year of the project was beneficial for both students and teachers, it was not without its challenges. Some teachers, particularly those who did not teach reading, found it difficult to implement peer coaching in their subject area. Moreover, the issue of time was a barrier for many teachers.

As the first year drew to a close, the leadership team reviewed the findings from the data at a Network workshop. Using this information, the team developed a revised action plan for the following year.

FOLLOWING UP IN THE SECOND YEAR

Based on the results of data collected during the first year of the action research project, the leadership team decided to broaden peer coaching to other areas of the curriculum during its second year. A lesson learned from the first year was the importance of allowing teachers to select a focus based on their needs. While the schoolwide focus remained on instruction, teachers could choose to participate in various interest areas (e.g., science, reading, writing, social studies, and math). School Improvement Cadres (SIC), teams of approximately six to eight teachers, met monthly to focus on content-specific needs. The SIC meetings began early in the year and took the place of a regularly scheduled faculty meeting. This helped alleviate some of the time constraints that had posed a challenge during the first year. A facilitator from each group shared results of monthly meetings with the action research leadership team.

Each SIC determined its own action research focus for the year. For example, the Reading SIC focused on improving vocabulary instruction. Throughout the year, the group shared effective teaching strategies related to vocabulary instruction that could be implemented schoolwide. In addition, they established peer-coaching partnerships with other members of the SIC and observed reading instruction in each others' classrooms. Ultimately, the goal for all of the SICs was to involve the whole faculty in action research that was relevant to their perceived needs.

Our case study of the first year of action research at Gonzales demonstrates that a new school can effectively conduct action research. In fact, maybe the very beginning of a school's existence is the time to establish a culture of inquiry. Sergiovanni (quoted in Poetter, 1997), in reference to novice teachers, states "Inquiry from the beginning is not only a good idea, but a doable one" (p. x). As the Gonzales action research project demonstrates, he could have been referring to new schools as well.

CONCLUDING THOUGHTS

As we have discussed, this collaborative project resulted in positive outcomes for the Gonzales faculty and students. The authors benefited as well. In reflecting on the experience, we share what we as individuals learned from participating in this school–university collaboration.

Barbara

Barbara explains how the role of critical friend was uncomfortable for her:

> At first, I didn't like being called a "critical friend." The term "critical" seemed negative—placing me in a judgmental or evaluative role. However, as I began working with the School Improvement Network and the Gonzales Elementary School leadership team, I realized the concept of critical friend was far more encompassing than my narrow definition. My role involved much more than critiquing the school's action research efforts.

Barbara goes on to share how she served as a support person for the leadership team:

> *The leadership team was highly motivated. At times, I wondered if they needed me. However, I felt my greatest contribution was serving as a liaison between the university and the school. I was able to provide additional resources, such as coordinating efforts of graduate students, searching the literature related to peer coaching, helping with data collection and analysis procedures, and assisting with grant writing.*

Observing firsthand the impact of peer coaching on the implementation of guided reading gave Barbara greater insight into the effectiveness of this strategy. As a teacher educator, she has been able to share this knowledge in her work with novice and experienced teachers.

Iris

Iris was working on her master's degree in Educational Administration during the action research project. She credits her participation as a teacher-leader in the collaborative action research with helping her develop as an instructional leader. She states: "Taking a leadership role in the action research project helped me develop a broader perspective on the school environment. No longer is it just *my classroom*; I now view myself as one part of *our school*." Participating in action research also helped Iris realize the importance of collecting data to inform her teaching. "You not only have to think about what you are teaching, but what the data (formal and informal) reveal about your students' performance."

Moreover, peer coaching helped Iris build positive relationships with other teachers. She explains:

> *Action research and peer coaching enabled me to step outside of my own classroom. Engaging in meaningful conversations with other colleagues led to a sharing of ideas that improved my teaching. I learned to hear others' thoughts on my teaching and not take it as criticism, but as a learning experience—a way to see it through fresh eyes. Ultimately, it helped me get to know other teachers in positive and professional ways.*

In sum, Barbara and Iris grew professionally as a result of participating in this collaborative project. They both agree that their involvement helped them gain a greater insight into the power of university–school collaborations to influence schoolwide improvement.

What We've Learned

Suggestions for Universities and Schools

Stephen P. Gordon

Steve Gordon coordinated the School Improvement Network.

WE HOPE that each of the chapters in this book has provided useful information to universities considering establishing action research networks and to PK–12 schools considering schoolwide action research. This final chapter consolidates what we in the School Improvement Network have learned into suggestions for universities and schools. Some of these suggestions come from our successes, others from our failures. We focus here on general suggestions that can be used by networks and schools as they organize for action research in a variety of different ways.

SUGGESTIONS FOR UNIVERSITIES

Our suggestions here relate to forming true partnerships, considering and fostering school readiness, establishing personal relationships, providing university-based assistance, providing on-site assistance, helping schools initiate action research, helping schools implement action research, and critiquing university involvement.

Form True Partnerships

One characteristic of true partnership is that each partner receives something valuable from the partnership that would not otherwise be available. Thus, it is important that action research networks be structured so that both the sponsoring university and the participating schools receive significant benefits. Moreover, the university and school are only the largest partners. Professors who coordinate the network or serve as critical friends, graduate students, principals, teacher-leaders, and regular classroom teachers are all partners in school improvement, and all should benefit from the partnership. For example, networks can be structured so that professors serving as critical friends are provided course releases, opportunities for publication, and learning activities for their students. Benefits to teachers might include learning new teaching skills, opportunities for leadership, an improved work environment, and—most importantly—improved student learning.

Another characteristic of a true partnership is equality of the partners. In the traditional university–school partnership, the university is the senior partner and the school is the junior partner. Real partnership, however, means both equal status and equal decision-making power. What was said earlier about partner benefits applies to partner equality as well; in true partnerships, not only are the organizations (university and school) considered equals, but individuals and groups within the partner organizations also are treated as equals. One of our more interesting findings regarding the more successful Network schools, for example, was that teachers in these schools reported that they were treated as equals by school administrators during meetings about the school's action research.

Partnership, of course, involves equal responsibility as well as an equal role in decision-making. Those Network schools that did not devote sufficient time and energy to the decision-making process, or consider their teachers to be equal players in decision-making, also contributed less to the Network and were less successful with action research.

Consider and Assist with School Readiness

Some of the schools in the Network simply were not ready to engage in schoolwide action research. As discussed by Gordon et al. in Chapter 5 and by McGhee and Boone in Chapter 6, there are a variety of reasons why a school may not be ready. Authoritarian leadership, low teacher commitment, the absence of an infrastructure for teacher collaboration, and the lack of a collective school vision are all indicators of low readiness. Other organizational barriers such as a negative school culture, lack of time, and school size may hinder readiness. One approach a university can take is to look for the presence of barriers to readiness and simply not form partnerships with schools possessing several barriers. However, considering that the whole purpose of the action research network is to help schools improve—and schools lacking readiness probably need more assistance than others—simply "weeding out" schools that are not ready seems counterproductive.

A more constructive approach when working with schools with low readiness would be to add a new *readiness phase* to the beginning of the action research process. In the readiness phase, for example, professional development on democratic leadership could be provided to school leaders, or teachers could receive professional development on the process and benefits of action research. The network also could help the school develop an infrastructure for communication and collaboration, or assist the school through a process for developing a collective vision. Yet another type of assistance that could be provided during a readiness phase is the development of a core group of teacher-leaders who could assist school administrators in facilitating action research. Once a satisfactory level of readiness is achieved, the school can begin its journey through the action research cycle described in the Introduction with a much better chance of success.

Establish Personal Relationships

Good working relationships between universities and schools are based on good personal relationships between individuals from both settings. Guajardo (Chapter 1) recalls several visits to the school he was assigned to for informal discussions with administrators and teachers prior to the initiation of action research. Nelson (Chapter 2) discusses resisting the urge for action, choosing to first take time to build relationships with members of a school's action research leadership team. Slater (Chapter 3) reports asking principals to visit his university classes to establish relationships with the graduate students who would assist with action research. Ross (Chapter 8) believes that her experience as a middle school teacher and administrator as well as activities at early Network meetings fostered a "positive connection" with the school she assisted.

Many of the connections fostered by the Network became long-term personal and professional relationships. Critical friends and veteran principals within the Network became mentors to younger principals. Critical friends and teachers also developed long-term relationships. For example, critical friend Davis and teacher-leader Escandón (the co-authors of Chapter 9) became writing partners. Although they often took considerable time to develop, personal relationships became the heart and soul of Network and school success.

Provide University-Based Assistance

We found it valuable to bring action research leadership teams from different schools and districts together at the university on a regular basis (approximately every two months). We recommend that universities sponsoring action research do this. In fact, we suggest that network meetings be held on campus even more often—perhaps eight times across the school year, with each meeting a whole-day affair.

Early on, leadership teams need to gain a thorough understanding of the concepts and principles underlying action research. There are seven phases in the action research model presented in the Introduction (Figure I.1)—eight phases if a readiness phase is needed—and there are no *easy* phases in action research. Leadership teams need to develop knowledge and skills in each phase, plan each phase, and reflect on the activities and effects of each phase. More network meetings, spread across the school year, would allow teams to reflect at each meeting on their past or current phase of action research, participate in in-depth learning about the next phase, and develop plans for leading the school through that next phase. The reflection and planning activities suggested here are critical because administrators and teacher-leaders have so little time for reflection and planning during (or before, or after) the typical school day. A sufficient number of network meetings provided by the sponsoring university gives leadership teams the gifts of space (from the hectic schedules, problems, and stress of the school day) and time. The university setting, interesting presenters, a nice lunch, and interaction with like-minded educators from other schools and districts—all of these help educators with the hard work of leading schoolwide action research.

Learning about, reflecting on, and planning for action research all benefit from discussion among teams from different schools. Time should be reserved for teams from different schools to share goals, data, problems, and possible solutions. Whole-group discussions and Q&A sessions also can assist learning. Discussion within and among teams is enhanced when critical friends attend the meetings and join in these discussions.

We recommend that additional forms of university-based support be considered by action research networks. Graduate classes can help to gather and analyze data, prepare reviews of literature on a school's focus area, and so forth. It is important that graduate student participation be well structured and monitored. It is equally important that the graduate students' work provide real benefits to the schools they are working with, while resulting in academic growth for the graduate students. If the university has been awarded a grant to support the network, it is surprising how much network schools appreciate even small sub-grants to assist them with their action research. Finally, inviting network schools to present their action research at network-sponsored conferences open to other educators provides the schools recognition as well as an opportunity to share their research with a wider professional audience.

Provide On-Site Assistance

One suggestion for on-site assistance is a whole-school session on the principles and process of action research, provided by the school's critical friend or another university faculty member. This presentation should increase the chances of buy-in by the school community. Minimally, it will give the school the information it needs to decide whether it wishes to proceed with action research.

The critical friend is the most important provider of on-site assistance. Professors and others need to be made aware of the critical friend's role and responsibilities before they agree to be critical friends. Critical friends new to the role, no matter how expert, should be provided an orientation to the network, the specific model of action research used by the network, and the school they will be working with.

Critical friends for the School Improvement Network agreed to visit their assigned schools four times a year (twice a semester), but many friends visited their school far more often. We now suggest that critical friends visit their schools once a month. It is vital that critical friends establish credibility with school administrators and teachers at the beginning of their work with the school. We found that different schools engaging in action research have different support needs, which means that critical friends need to be flexible, shaping the assistance they provide to fit their assigned school's needs. Critical friends need to balance their support between university and school, between scientific rigor and practicality, and between school administrators and teachers. Finally, as suggested by Nelson (Chapter 2), critical friends should *simultaneously* support and challenge their assigned school.

Schools doing action research usually need assistance with one or more innovations (a new curriculum, a new teaching method, and so on) as well as with the action research process. If the critical friend does not have the expertise to provide assistance with a particular innovation, we recommend that the sponsoring university tap into its faculty resources and provide an expert to visit the school to consult with administrators and teachers, deliver training, and so on. When this is done, the critical friend can assume the role of liaison between the school and the university specialist.

Provide Special Support for Initiation

No matter how well the action research project is explained at a network meeting, no matter how many case studies of successful action research are shared, no matter how much initial enthusiasm is expressed by administrators and teachers, schools have difficulty getting their first action research project off the ground. All of the Network schools—including those that became high performance schools—had various levels of difficulty organizing for and initiating action research. Experience has taught us that there is a large gap between understanding action research on a conceptual level and being able to *do* action research in a P–12 school.

In the early stages of action research, schools need highly structured assistance. One form of such assistance used by both Guajardo (Chapter 1) and Slater (Chapter 4) is providing schools with discussion questions that will help members of the school community reflect on their values, beliefs, vision, and needs. Although it is up to the school to determine its own focus area, schools appreciate assistance in developing instruments to gather preliminary data and in analyzing those data. They also value assistance in setting up discussion groups to review data and reach consensus on a focus area.

Once the focus area has been identified, the school needs assistance with a new round of (target) data gathering and analysis and discussion aimed at developing an action plan. Reviews of literature (usually including both an executive summary and the full review) can be provided to schools by the network, and schools can use both target data and reviews of literature as input for their action plan. Slater and his graduate students (Chapter 4) went so far as to provide schools with information on alternative actions for consideration.

Once the school has made decisions on what innovations to include in its action plan, the school's critical friend might introduce Stiegelbauer's questions to consider in the initiation phase, including questions about people, the innovation, putting change in place, and supports (Chapter 7). Another idea, used by Guajardo and his graduate students (Chapter 1), is to suggest an action research model tailored to the school's particular focus area. A tailored model is more context specific and provides more structure than generic action research models found in the literature, but still allows the school to make its own decisions at each step of the process. Action research leadership teams should be provided ample time during network meetings for planning initiation, with detailed feedback from university professors. Critical friends should be present to provide direct assistance at both network and school meetings dealing with initiation.

Provide Special Support for Implementation

The Network defined *implementation* as all activities between initiation and the time when improvement activities became embedded within the school culture. In the Network, the wheel spinners really never got beyond the initiation stage. The coasters made it into the implementation stage and experienced implementation success during the first year, but lost momentum during the second year. The high performance schools successfully initiated and implemented action research, and were in the continuation stage at the end of their relationship with the Network.

It is important that regular network meetings continue during the implementation stage. Schools need help with providing professional development for teachers, assisting and monitoring improvement activities, and conducting annual program evaluations and revisions. On-site support by the critical friend throughout implementation is vital. The critical friend can provide consultation to the action research leadership team and faculty, and can assist teacher-leaders who are providing demonstration lessons, facilitating study groups, coordinating peer coaching, and so on. The critical friend can give practitioners encouragement during difficult times, challenge them to improve when implementation begins to wane, and provide positive feedback when implementation is going well.

In our work with Network schools we found that the "implementation dip" described by many scholars is a very real phenomenon (indeed, we can say that coasters experienced implementation dips from which they never recovered). The best way to deal with the implementation dip is to let schools know it is coming and help them develop strategies to deal with the dip when it arrives. We suggest an entire workshop on dealing with the implementation dip at the beginning of the second year of action research. In this workshop, action research leadership teams can be presented with typical implementation problems and coping strategies. As leadership teams begin to experience specific problems with implementation, they can work with other network schools and their critical friends to address those problems. Stiegelbauer's questions on implementation (Chapter 7) can be the basis for regular discussions on implementation at network meetings and during visits by critical friends.

Engage in Self-Critique

Smyth's work (Chapter 4) encourages two types of self critique by universities and professors engaged in school research: micro and macro. On the micro level, Smyth invites us to critique our relationships with the schools we do research with. Whose interests are being served? Are we engaged in authentic collaboration with schools? Is our work transforming school cultures and promoting social justice? Are we treating school practitioners ethically and respectfully?

On the macro level, Smyth asks us to critically examine the whole concept of the professoriate's role in educational research. Is the collaborative action research we are engaged in relevant to the educational community at large? Is the research we participate in contributing to an emancipatory knowledge base with the capacity to improve education and society? Are we communicating that knowledge base to the larger educational community in ways it can be understood? Are we connecting collaborative action research to the pursuit of academic freedom?

SUGGESTIONS FOR SCHOOLS

Our suggestions for schools considering schoolwide action research include understanding the potential of and necessary commitment to action research, using democratic leadership, joining an action research partnership or network, encouraging teacher leadership and participation, considering diversity, providing time and other resources, managing the change process, taking a long-term view, and providing opportunities for recognition, sharing, and celebration.

Understand the Potential of and Necessary Commitment to Action Research

The high performance schools in the School Improvement Network showed us the enormous potential of action research to help schools reach their improvement goals and transform their cultures. Readings on action research, visits to schools with successful projects, and visiting panels including professors and practitioners engaged in collaborative action research all can help a school community understand the potential of action research.

Knowing about the potential of action research, however, provides practitioners with only part of the information they need. They also need to know that for action research to work it must become a high priority for the school community, because it requires the expenditure of considerable time and energy over a period of years. Action research, in short, is hard work. Unless the school can connect action research to high priority needs that it is determined to meet, the research is unlikely to ever reach a stage where it is leading to school improvement or the enhancement of student learning. An understanding of the potential of action research goes hand in hand with an understanding of the commitment it requires; as a school community realizes the commitment required, it is unlikely to make that commitment unless the potential benefits are clearly visualized.

Use Democratic Leadership

Based on our experiences with the Network, principals leading schoolwide action research are most successful using a democratic leadership style. As discussed in Chapter 5, the two-way communication, collaboration, and open inquiry that characterize schoolwide action research cannot thrive under authoritarian leadership. As suggested by Glickman et al. (2007), democratic school governance and schoolwide action research are really two sides of the same coin. Democratic leadership of action research is actualized in a number of ways, including

- Allowing all members of the school community to investigate the potential benefits and required commitments of schoolwide action research, and to participate in the decision about whether to proceed with action research
- Involving all members of the school community in the selection of a focus area for action research
- Allowing all members of the school community input into the school's action plan
- Implementing action research in a way that will allow teachers and other professionals choices in their own practice as they work to help the school meet collective improvement goals
- Providing members of the school community opportunities to raise concerns, make suggestions, and request assistance as the action plan is carried out
- Involving all members of the school community in a formal, annual evaluation of the action research program

Collaborative action research involves a variety of different types of meetings: for study, planning, data analysis, problem-solving, and so forth. These meetings often are attended by individuals in different roles, such as school administrators, teachers, parents, professors, and graduate students. One sign of democracy in action research is the presence of symmetrical relationships among those attending the meetings. In the words of teachers from high performance schools, "everyone is equal" and "there are no bosses, just professionals working together."

Join an Action Research Partnership or Network

It will be no surprise to the reader that we urge schools interested in school-wide action research to seek out a university partner or a university-sponsored action research network. Most universities with good-sized colleges of education have professors who are interested in working with schools and who have expertise in action research. University professors can provide schools with training on action research and ongoing assistance as the action research project develops. Assistance with data gathering, data analysis, planning, and the change process seem to be the most critical types of assistance schools need. We have a bias, of course, for our own model, which includes periodic meetings for action research leadership teams, critical friends who provide on-site technical and moral support, assistance provided by graduate classes, and mini-grants to assist schools with planning, implementation, and assessment.

Although partnership with a university can be very valuable, we encourage schools that can to join a university-sponsored action research network. Network membership, if it includes regular network meetings, has the advantage of action research leadership teams from different districts and schools meeting together to share ideas, compare experiences, and provide mutual support. Network membership means that—in addition to professors from the sponsoring university serving as critical friends—network schools' leadership teams can serve as critical friends to one another. Network membership opens up all kinds of possibilities, such as schools sharing research strategies, interschool visits, and cross-school mentoring.

Encourage Teacher Leadership and Participation

Schoolwide action research is too complicated and too dependent on teacher involvement for school administrators to lead all by themselves. Teacher leadership is required, first in the form of teacher-leaders on the school's action research leadership team, and eventually expanding to include large numbers of teachers in various leadership roles. Although not every teacher in the school needs to assume a formal leadership role, efforts should be made to have as many teachers as possible *participate* in schoolwide action research. As a general rule, the more teacher participation, the more teacher buy-in, and the greater the chances for success. Teacher leadership and involvement should be sought in each phase of action research:

- More highly involved teachers can help design and administer data gathering tools, and create data summaries. Other teachers can complete surveys, participate in interviews, and so on, and join collegial groups that review data and discuss implications.
- More highly involved teachers can lead study groups that examine alternative foci and goals for action research, and other teachers can participate in those study groups.
- More highly involved teachers can help to write action plans, and other teachers can provide input for action plans, provide feedback on drafts of action plans, and vote on approval of formal plans.
- During implementation, more involved teachers can lead grade-level, vertical, curriculum development, instructional support, or community relations teams, and other teachers can serve on those teams. More involved teachers can deliver workshops, teach demonstration lessons, or coordinate peer coaching, and other teachers can attend workshops, observe demonstration lessons, and participate in peer coaching.

Teachers who initially do not participate in action research—or who engage in token participation—eventually can be won over by observing active participation by teachers who value action research and report positive classroom effects. Nothing increases participation like success! School leaders should continuously look for teachers who have become ready to assume leadership of action research, and should find leadership roles for such teachers. Schools that experience success during the first year of action research often expand their focus area for the second year, which in turn provides additional opportunities for teacher leadership.

Consider Diversity

Shifting demographics in the United States means that increasing numbers of minority students are attending public schools across the nation. The growing diversity of our nation and our schools is a factor that needs to be considered while planning for action research. There often is a mismatch between the culture of minority students and the culture of the schools they attend. Action research can focus on matters of cultural competence and cultural responsiveness, or can integrate attention to diversity with other types of research. Actually, it is difficult to imagine any school improvement effort that would not need to take cultural diversity into account. Even those schools with few or no racial or ethnic minorities have other types of diversity, and all schools have a responsibility to prepare their students to live in a culturally diverse society. Thus, regardless of the school population or focus area, attention to cultural diversity ought to be a component of any action research project.

Provide Time and Other Resources

Our work with the Network verified the experiences of others that the number one resource needed by practitioners doing action research is time. Time was a barrier for all Network schools. The more successful schools, however, found ways to get around or climb over the time barrier. The least successful schools viewed the time problem as insurmountable. Ross (Chapter 8) describes how the district she worked with as critical friend found ways to give teachers working on action research "the gift of time." Providing substitute teachers, using faculty meetings to work on action research rather than information items, and restructuring the school schedule are a few ways to provide time for action research. Murphy (1997, 1999) and Darling-Hammond (1999) suggest a variety of additional ways to provide teachers time for collaborative work.

Action research projects, of course, differ in the types of human and material resources they require, and schools vary in the resources they have available. However, if a school's action research is focused on the school's priority needs, then it makes sense to concentrate available resources on the action research. Funding for action research is most frequently needed for professional development, teacher-release time, and instructional resources and materials. Schools should consider applying for external grants to support their action research projects. Ironically, in this age of "science-based education," external funding for action research per se is not readily available. However, schoolwide action research usually has at its center an innovation intended to improve student achievement, and external funding may be available if the school emphasizes the innovation itself in funding proposals. As discussed earlier, some action research networks are themselves funded by external grants and can use some of their funding to award subgrants to network schools.

Manage the Change Process

We have already discussed one key to effectively managing the change process, which is to involve all members of the school community in decisions about change. Another key is to build continuous feedback into the action research. All action research needs to be periodically modified (sometimes radically), and the school needs feedback to know what modifications to make. This feedback can come from ongoing data gathering and analysis, critical friends, teachers, students, and parents. Provision of feedback, of course, must be accompanied by sufficient flexibility to make necessary changes in the action research process and school improvement activities. As has been noted by many change experts, the change process is a learning process and should be managed accordingly. A related lesson learned from the Network schools is the need to keep action research dynamic and growing. It is interesting, for example, that the high performance Network schools significantly expanded the scope of their action research in its second year.

Based on her work with Network schools as well as a number of other projects, Stiegelbauer (Chapter 7) provides additional insights about managing change. These suggestions are consistent with a wide body of literature on school change (see, for example, Fullan, 1999, 2001a, 2001b; Fullan & Miles, 1992; Hall & Hord, 2001; Hord, 2004):

- Change should be neither too large nor too small.
- Significant change involves more than adoption of an innovation. Meaningful change involves change in beliefs, values, traditions, behaviors, skills, and relationships.
- Change needs to be simple to understand, practical, relevant to local needs, and adaptable to local contexts. Change also needs to have clear benefits, especially to students.
- Individuals respond differently to change and go through developmental stages regarding change.
- Those expected to implement change need a map for going through the change process.
- The change process itself goes through different stages—initiation, implementation, and continuation or renewal—and different plans, resources, and support roles are needed for each stage.
- The best support for change results from relationships that develop within the change effort that lead to growth and development.
- The broader goal of any change effort is to develop an organizational capacity for change in response to a changing environment.

The last point in the list above leads us into a discussion of the need to take a long-term view of action research.

Take a Long-Term View

The immediate goal of action research is to solve a concrete school problem or achieve a concrete school improvement goal. However, school leaders must keep in mind that action research also has a long-term goal, a goal even more important than the immediate purpose of any action research project. Different writers have described this larger goal in different ways, but there clearly is a commonality among the descriptions. I call this long-range goal *a culture of continuous improvement,* but others have referred to the goal as:

- The school as the center of inquiry (Schaefer, 1967)
- The self renewing school (Joyce, Wolf, & Calhoun, 1993)
- Internal school development (Fullan, 2000)
- Schools that learn (Senge et al., 2000)
- Schools as inquiring communities (Calhoun, 2002)
- Professional learning communities (Hord, 2004)

To take this long-term goal seriously means that school leaders need to view each phase of an action research project through a "dual lens." Through one lens, they view the progress of a current action research project in solving an immediate problem; through the other lens, they view the current action research as a step in the development of a culture of continuous improvement in which teachers, staff, and students have made inquiry, reflection, dialogue, democracy, and collaboration a way of life.

Provide for Recognition, Sharing, and Celebration

Teachers and others involved in action research should be recognized for their hard work and progress. They can be recognized at faculty meetings, by being given leadership roles, with release time to work on the action research, and so forth. Individuals and groups can share their experiences with action research at faculty meetings, during open houses, and so on, but they also should be provided opportunities to share their work with a larger professional community. For example, schools can share the progress of their action research by developing school portfolios documenting their research projects. Electronic portfolios can be placed on the school's or action research network's website and be available to anyone. Another advantage of electronic school portfolios is that they can be continuously updated.

In our experience, schools begin to see the fruits of their action research (improved school cultures, teaching, and student learning) toward the end of the project's second year. This is a good time for school teams to submit articles on their action research to educational journals or deliver presentations on the research at district, network, state, or national conferences. Presenting at conferences serves the dual purposes of recognition and sharing.

Although a school should celebrate successes in action research throughout the school year, the end of the school year is a great time to have a schoolwide celebration of what has been accomplished. A year-end celebration provides additional opportunities for individuals and groups to share their work and be recognized, but it also provides school leaders an opportunity to show their appreciation for the researchers' hard work.

WE HAVE LEARNED MUCH from our association with Network schools that will help us do a better job of facilitating action research in the future. We hope the reader also will benefit from lessons we have learned.

Sample Literature Review

Miguel A. Guajardo

This is one of three brief literature reviews prepared for
San Joaquin High School by graduate students in
Miguel Guajardo's Campus Leadership course.

SCHOOL AND COMMUNITY LEADERSHIP

A CRUCIAL COMPONENT in a child's education is the involvement of parents and community in the school. As Tierney (2002) tells us, "In the early 20th century, in general, researchers assumed that the family actually caused harm to a child's educational welfare," but today educational philosophy "assumes that parents, siblings, and extended families play a central role," in students' educational progress (p. 589).

Despite agreement on the value of parental engagement, there is a discrepancy between how teachers and parents view parent involvement. According to a study of six high-performing schools in South Texas, teachers are looking for formal participation in school activities, such as PTA meetings, attending parent–teacher conferences, and volunteering, with a goal of enhancing student achievement, while parents prefer a more informal approach, including checking homework, sending children to school clean and rested, and encouraging them to stay in school (Scribner, Young, & Pedroza, 1999).

Many authors have written about the different ways educators try to connect with parents, such as soliciting their input, allowing them to share in the planning process, and honoring and respecting "the beliefs and values of families from culturally different backgrounds." Kalyanpur and Harry (1997) are quick to point out that, while these are good steps, they alone are not sufficient: "Professionals need to become aware of both the cultural basis of the services they offer and their own cultural assumptions" (p. 489).

Models for Engagement

Brooks and Kavanaugh (1999) identified three conceptual models for school–community relationships:

- Community as a Resource in which the community is seen as a source of funds, services, and volunteers;
- Traditional Community in which the school and staff are seen as integral parts of the community; and the
- Learning Community whose philosophy embraces continuous learning by all as necessary for the education of children.

Each model has a worldview and associated best practices. High-achieving schools fall into each of the three categories, but the Community as Resource model is most common.

Another model for parental engagement is provided by the Alliance Schools (Shirley, 1997). The Alliance Schools Initiative is a community-based program to increase student achievement in low-income areas throughout Texas. Since 1991, the Alliance Schools Initiative has focused on bringing parents together with teachers and community leaders to try to solve problems in schools, learn about school reform practices, and work together to address the needs of children and their families. The Alliance Schools Initiative is a partnership between the Texas Industrial Areas Foundation (TIAF) Network, the Interfaith Education Fund, and the Texas Education Agency (TEA). The initiative focuses on restructuring the relationship among stakeholders in school communities, including parents, teachers, school administrators, students, community and business leaders, and public officials. The Initiative teaches the art of communication—exchanging ideas, debate, and compromise—in order to change the culture of schools and neighborhoods.

The strategy used by this Initiative increases parental engagement, teacher morale, and student success at Alliance School campuses. Some methods used by Alliance Schools include

- Core teams, consisting of the principal, teachers, parents, and other community members, are trained to conduct house meetings where community members, parents, and school staff communicate their concerns and construct a plan of action for the school.
- Walk for Success, or neighborhood walks, where teachers, parents, church members, and administrators walk the streets of the neighborhood and engage parents in conversations about the school.

- School staff receives training to offer education, services, and training for parents and community leaders who participate in school reform efforts.
- A staff person keeps parents apprised of important dates and informs them of their children's scholastic performance.
- Parents learn how to help their children with homework.
- Other classes offered are based on needs identified by the parents themselves. Possible class choices include parenting skills, English as a Second Language, adult literacy, and computer literacy.

Cultural Responsiveness

The literature on high-performing schools tells us that "teachers adjust and adapt patterns of instruction to be more congruent with those of the children's home and community" (Newman & Roskos, 1994). They emphasize that parents are their children's first teachers and that an emphasis must be placed on identifying and valuing a child's cultural identity. Newman and Roskos define a culturally responsive approach as one which

- Acknowledges and appreciates children's home cultures and attempts to build upon the uses of language and literacy with which children are already familiar.
- Promotes collaboration among children and between children and adults as they learn through social interaction.
- Shares the same standards of achievement for children of diverse backgrounds as for those from the mainstream.

According to Kalyanpur and Harry (1997) there are three levels of cultural awareness: overt, covert, and subtle. Overt is an awareness of external differences such as language and manner of dress. Covert is awareness that is not immediately recognized externally, such as communication style. Finally, subtle awareness is the understanding of specific values and beliefs of a culture. Kalyanpur and Harry (1997) state, "The issue is not that we must have had the same experiences in terms of culture, ethnic background, race, socio-economic status, or gender, as the families we serve (because we cannot), but that we have the willingness to learn about and understand their experiences, that we are willing to understand how our own experiences have shaped us, and that we respect and accept these differences in our various experiences" (p. 506).

The posture of reciprocity as defined by Kalyanpur and Harry (1997) is a teacher orientation in which they "engage in explicit discussions with families regarding differential cultural values and practices, bringing to the interactions an openness of mind, the ability to be reflective in their practice, and to listen to the other perspective" (p. 498). Additionally, "they must respect the new body of knowledge that emerges from these discussions and make allowances for differences in perspective when responding to the family's need" (p. 498).

The four guidelines of the posture of reciprocity are identify cultural values, discover if the family recognizes these values or how they differ in understanding, recognize and give explicit respect, and discuss and collaborate. The key features of the posture of reciprocity are

- It goes beyond the awareness of differences to self-awareness— Relationships must be interactive and must be understanding of the different perspectives.
- It aims for subtle levels of awareness of differences—Understanding the underlying cultural values of professional and family responses—ask "WHY?"
- It has universal applicability—All perspectives must be heard and valued.
- It avoids stereotyping—Every situation is unique to each family.
- It ensures that both parents and professionals are empowered— Each party learns about the other through dialogue.

A possible approach to increasing cultural awareness and responsiveness is the development of ethnographic studies in which teachers or students go into the homes of students to conduct interviews of the family in order to gain a deeper understanding of their culture and home life. González and Moll (2002) believe that, "people are competent and have knowledge, and their life experiences have given them that knowledge." They call this "funds of knowledge." This type of interaction can lead to a more culturally responsive instructional approach.

The *Puente* Project is a program in Southern California that creates pathways or bridges between students and college. The program has five components:

- High school teachers providing intensive college-prep English classes on Latino literature in 9th and 10th grades
- Bicultural counselors guiding students toward college through high school
- Latino community professionals providing mentoring

- Families being involved with students' pathways to college
- Peer networks of *Puente* students who support each other's college goals

In this program teachers attempt to make connections between students' cultural background and their learning. Additionally, it is beneficial to have counselors that understand where students are coming from and how to help them move forward (Cooper, 2002). Tierney (2002) describes the program's cultural integrity, which he defines as calling "on students' racial and ethnic backgrounds as ways to enhance learning" (p. 599).

A study of South Texas schools also concluded that a culturally responsive pedagogy is a necessary element for the success of students. Scribner and Reyes (1999) identified five central themes:

- Teachers believe every student has the ability to achieve, and they communicate this belief to students, parents and colleagues.
- Teachers provide a caring environment in which students are viewed as the most valuable resources of the school.
- Teachers empower their students, providing opportunities for experimentation, innovation, discovery, and problem-solving.
- Teachers make use of two-way "instructional conversations" with students that encourage goal-directed activity and the use of higher order thinking skills on the part of students.
- Teachers use students' funds of knowledge as the basis of their instructional strategies.

Communication—Hidden Curriculum

Another important area to address is communication between schools and families with regard to programs that affect a student's educational career. Torrez (2004) states that "parents do not understand the importance of being an advocate in guiding their children through a high school curriculum that would be necessary to ensure their children's eligibility for college entrance" (p. 59). Tierney (2002) describes this as "cultural capital." According to Tierney (2002), cultural capital "is a set of linguistic and cultural competencies that children inherit from their families" (p. 592) that is not directly taught, yet understood among the social elites. This is not, however, happening among our culturally diverse learners. Therefore it is the school's responsibility to provide that knowledge to parents and students. In a survey conducted by Torrez (2004), some parents responded by stating, "They would be desirous of parent workshops to gather information concerning curriculum requirements, SAT preparation courses, and availability of financial aid" (p. 58).

Changing the school culture to encourage more transparent communication and the development of cultural capital for students and parents is especially difficult in secondary schools because of the number of students each teacher instructs and the number of teachers each student sees. Scribner et al. (1999) encourage personal, positive interaction by telephone or, preferably, in person; all formal communication in both English and Spanish; the use of academic teams; a school environment that is welcoming and well-labeled; and structures which provide for meaningful participation by parents in areas deemed important and relevant by them. They further encourage home visits as the most effective communication tool, citing six reasons: parents perceived home visits to be an extension of courtesy; parents often had young children at home; many parents did not have access to transportation; home visits indicated awareness of the community by staff members; home visits were viewed by parents as a form of caring; and home visits were a highly valued form of personal contact.

References

Achieve, Inc. (2005). *An action agenda for improving America's high schools.* Washington, DC: National Governor's Association.

Ainscow, M., & Southworth, G. (1996). School improvement: A study of the roles of leaders and external consultants. *School Effectiveness and School Improvement, 7*(3), 229–251.

Allen, L., & Calhoun, E. F. (1998). Schoolwide action research: Findings from six years of study. *Phi Delta Kappan, 79*(9), 706–710.

American Institutes for Research. (2005). *Executive summary: Evaluation of the Bill and Melinda Gates Foundation high school grants, 2001–2004.* Washington, DC: Author.

Anderson, G. L., & Herr, K. (1999). The new paradigm wars: Is there room for rigorous practitioner knowledge in schools and universities? *Educational Researcher, 28*(5), 12–40.

Baker, P. J. (2001). Michael Fullan's compelling vision of educational change: Cultivating meaningful relationships for all. *Planning and Changing, 32*(3&4), 2–17.

Bambino, D. (2002). Critical friends. *Educational Leadership, 59*(6), 25–27.

Barth, R. (2006). Improving relationships within the schoolhouse. *Educational Leadership, 63*(6), 8–13.

Beaver, J. (2001). *Developmental reading assessment.* Glenview, IL: Celebration Press/Addison-Wesley.

Bello, E. E. (2006). Initiating a collaborative action research project: From choosing a school to planning the work on an issue. *Educational Action Research, 14*(1), 3–21.

Berliner, D. (2002). Educational research: The hardest science of all. *Educational Researcher, 31*(8), 18–20.

Bond, R., & Paterson, L. (2005). Coming down from the ivory tower? Academics' civic and economic engagement with community. *Oxford Review of Education, 31*(3), 331–351.

Botstein, L. (1997). *Jefferson's children: Education and the promise of American culture.* New York: Doubleday.

Boyer, E. (1990). *Scholarship reconsidered: Priorities of the professoriate.* Princeton, NJ: The Carnegie Foundation for the Advancement of Teaching.

Boyer, E. (1996). The scholarship of engagement. *The Journal of Public Service and Outreach, 1*(1), 11–20.

Bridgeland, J., Dilulio, J., & Morison, K. (2006). *The silent epidemic: Perspectives of high school dropouts.* Washington, DC: Civic Enterprises for the Bill and Melinda Gates Foundation.

Brooks, A. K., & Kavanaugh, P. C. (1999). Empowering the surrounding community. In P. Reyes, J. D. Scribner, & A. P. Scribner (Eds.), *Lessons from high-performing Hispanic schools: Creating learning communities* (pp. 61–93). New York: Teachers College Press.

Brown, E. D. (Ed.). (1996). *Breaking ranks: Changing an American institution.* Reston, VA: National Association of Secondary School Principals.

Calabrese, R. L. (2002). *The leadership assignment: Creating change.* Boston: Allyn & Bacon.

Calderwood, P. (2003). Toward a professional community for social justice. *Journal of Transformative Education, 1*(4), 301–320.

Calhoun, E. (1992). *How to conduct collaborative action research.* Alexandria, VA: Association for Supervision and Curriculum Development.

Calhoun, E. (1994). *How to use action research in a self-renewing school.* Alexandra, VA: Association for Supervision and Curriculum Development.

Calhoun, E. F. (2002). Action research for school improvement. *Educational Leadership, 59*(6), 18–24.

Calhoun, E. (2004). *Using data to assess your reading program.* Alexandria, VA: Association for Supervision and Curriculum Development.

Calhoun, E. F., & Allen, L. (1994, April). *Results of schoolwide action research in the League of Professional Schools.* Paper presented at the annual meeting of the American Educational Research Association, New Orleans, LA.

Chenoweth, T. G., & Everhart, R. B. (2002). *Navigating comprehensive school change: A guide for the perplexed.* Larchmont, NY: Eye on Education.

Clark, C., Moss, P., Goering, S., Herter, P., Lamar, B., Leonard, D., et al. (1996). Collaboration as dialogue: Teachers and researchers engage in a conversation and professional development. *American Educational Research Journal, 33*(1), 193–231.

Coalition of Essential Schools. (2000). *CES benchmarks.* Oakland, CA: CES National.

Collins, D. (Executive Producer), Niland, M. (Producer), & Carney, J. (Writer/Director). (2007). *Once* [Motion picture]. Ireland: Fox Searchlight.

Collinson, V., Cook, & T. F. (2007). *Organizational learning: Improving learning, teaching, and leading in school systems.* Thousand Oaks, CA: Sage Publications.

Cooper, C. R. (2002). Five bridges along students' pathways to college: A developmental blueprint of families, teachers, counselors, mentors, and peers in the Puente Project. *Educational Policy, 16,* 607–622.

Costa, A. L., & Kallick, B. (1993). Through the lens of a critical friend. *Educational Leadership,* 49–51.

Crandall, D. P., Eiseman, J. W., & Seashore Louis, K. (1986). Strategic planning issues that bear on the success of school improvement efforts. *Educational Administration Quarterly, 22*(3), 21–53.

Crawford, P. A., & Cornett, J. (2000). Looking back to find a vision: Exploring the emancipatory potential of teacher research. *Childhood Education, 77*(1), 37–40.

Cuban, L. (1988). A fundamental puzzle of school reform. *Phi Delta Kappan, 70*(5), 341–344.

Cuban, L. (2007). No more magical thinking: Leading from top or bottom. *School Administrator, 64*(3), 6.

Daniels, H., Bizar, M., & Zemelman, S. (2001). *Rethinking high school: Best practice in teaching, learning, and leadership.* Portsmouth, NH: Heinemann.

Danielson, C. (2002). *Enhancing student achievement: A framework for school improvement.* Alexandria, VA: Association for Supervision and Curriculum Development.

Darling-Hammond, L. (1999). Target time toward teachers. *Journal of Staff Development, 20*(2), 31–36.

Darling-Hammond, L. (2002). *Redesigning schools: What matters and what works.* Stanford, CA: School Redesign Network.

Darling-Hammond, L. (2003). Keeping good teachers: Why it matters and what leaders can do. *Educational Leadership, 60*(8), 6–13.

Diaz-Maggioli, G. (2004). *Teacher-centered professional development.* Alexandria, VA: Association for Supervision and Curriculum Development.

Donaldson, G. (2006). *Cultivating leadership in schools: Connecting people, purpose & practice.* New York: Teachers College Press.

DuFour, R. (2004). What is a professional learning community? *Educational Leadership, 61*(8), 6–11.

DuFour, R., Eaker, R., & DuFour, R. (2005). Introduction. In R. DuFour, R. Eaker, & R. DuFour (Eds.), *On common ground: The power of professional learning communities* (pp. 1–6). Bloomington, IN: Solution Tree.

Eisner, E. W. (2003). Questionable assumptions about schooling. *Phi Delta Kappan, 84*(9), 648–657.

Erickson, F. (2005). Arts, humanities, and sciences in educational research and social engineering in federal education policy. *Teachers College Record, 107*(1), 4–9.

Erickson, F., & Gutierrez, K. (2002). Culture, rigor, and science in educational research. *Educational Researcher, 31*(8), 21–24.

Fals-Borda, O., & Rahman, M. (1991). *Action and knowledge: Breaking the monopoly with participatory action research.* New York: Apex Press.

Fear, F., Rosaen, C., Bawden, R., & Foster-Fishman, D. (2006). *Coming to critical engagement: An autoethnographic exploration.* Lanham, MD: University Press of America.

Ferrero, D. J. (2005). Does 'research based' mean 'value neutral'? *Phi Delta Kappan, 86*(6), 425–432.

Frey, L., Pearce, W., Pollock, M., Artz, L., & Murphy, B. (1996). Looking for social justice in all the wrong places: On a communication approach to social justice. *Communication Studies, 47*(1&2), 110–127.

Fullan, M. (1985). Change processes and strategies at the local level. *Elementary School Journal, 84*(3), 391–420.

Fullan, M. (1991). *Overcoming barriers to educational change.* Paper commissioned by the Office of the Under Secretary of the U.S. Department of Education for the New American Schools Development Corporation Initiative. Washington, DC: U.S. Department of Education.

Fullan, M. (1999). *Change forces: The sequel.* Philadelphia: Taylor & Francis.

Fullan, M. (2000). The three stories of education reform. *Phi Delta Kappan, 81*(8), 581–584.

Fullan, M. (2001a). *Leading in a culture of change.* San Francisco: Jossey-Bass.

Fullan, M. (2001b). *The new meaning of educational change* (3rd ed.). New York: Teachers College Press.

Fullan, M. (2002). The change leader. *Educational Leadership, 59*(8), 16–20.

Fullan, M. G., & Hargreaves, A. (1992). *What's worth fighting for: Working together for your school.* Toronto: Ontario Public School Teachers' Federation.

Fullan, M. G., & Miles, M. B. (1992). Getting reform right: What works and what doesn't. *Phi Delta Kappan, 73*(10), 744–752.

Galbraith, P., & Anstrom, K. (1995, Spring). Peer coaching: An effective staff development model for educators of linguistically and culturally diverse students. *Directions in Language & Education, 1*(3). Retrieved May 9, 2008, from http://www.ncela.gwu.edu/pubs/directions/03.htm

Gardner, S. (2004). Participatory action research helps now. *Education Digest, 70*(3), 51–55.

George, A., Hall, G., & Stiegelbauer, S. (2006). *Measuring implementation in schools: The stage of concern questionnaire.* Austin, TX: Southwest Educational Development Laboratory.

Glanz, J. (1998). *Action research: An educational leader's guide to school improvement.* Norwood, MA: Christopher-Gordon.

Glickman, C. D. (1993). *Renewing America's schools: A guide for school-based action.* San Francisco: Jossey-Bass.

Glickman, C. D. (2002). *Leadership for learning: How to help teachers succeed.* Alexandria, VA: Association for Supervision and Curriculum Development.

Glickman, C. D., Gordon, S. P., & Ross-Gordon, J. M. (2007). *SuperVision and instructional leadership: A developmental approach* (7th ed.). Boston: Allyn & Bacon.

Goleman, D., Boyatzis, R., & McKee, A. (2002). *Primal leadership: Realizing the power of emotional intelligence.* Boston: Harvard Business School Publishing.

González, N., & Moll, L. C. (2002). *Cruzando el puente*: Building bridges to funds of knowledge. *Educational Policy, 16*, 623–641.

Gordon, S. P. (1999). Ready? How effective schools know it's time to take the plunge. *Journal of Staff Development, 20*(1), 48–53.

Gordon, S. (2006, November). *Action research for school improvement: Spreading seeds.* Paper presented at the annual convention of the University Council for Educational Administration (UCEA), San Antonio, TX.

Gordon, S., Butters, J., Maxey, S., & Ciccarelli, J. (2002). *Facilitator's guide: Improving instruction through observation and feedback.* Alexandria, VA: Association for Supervision and Curriculum Development.

Gordon, S., Stiegelbauer, S., & Diehl, J. (2006). Year One of school improvement: Examples from nine schools. *Educational Considerations, 23*(2), 17–29.

Greenwood, D. J., & Levin, M. (2007). *Introduction to action research: Social research for social change* (2nd ed.). Thousand Oaks, CA: Sage Publications.

Guajardo, M. A. (2002). *Education for leadership development: Preparing a new generation of leaders.* Doctoral dissertation, University of Texas, Austin. Retrieved May 9, 2008, from http://hdl.handle.net/2152/105

Guajardo, M. A., & Guajardo, F. J. (2002). Critical ethnography and community change. In Y. Zou and H. T. Trueba (Eds.), *Ethnography and schools: Qualitative approaches to the study of education* (pp. 291–304). Lanham, MD: Rowman & Littlefield.

Guajardo, M. A., Guajardo, F. J., & Casaperalta, E. (2008). Transformative education: Chronicling a pedagogy for social change. *Anthropology and Education Quarterly, 39*(1), 3–22.

Halbert, J., & Kaser, L. (2002). Inquiry, eh? School improvement through a network of inquiry. *Education Canada, 42*(2), 19.

Hall, G. E., & Hord, S. M. (1987). *Change in schools: Facilitating the process.* Albany: State University of New York Press.

Hall, G. E., & Hord, S. M. (2001). *Implementing change: Patterns, principles, and potholes.* Boston: Allyn & Bacon.

Hall, G., & Hord, S. (2006). *Implementing change: Patterns, principles and potholes* (2nd ed.). Boston: Allyn & Bacon.

Hall, G. E., & Loucks, S. F. (1977). A developmental model for determining whether the treatment is actually implemented. *American Educational Research Journal, 14*(3), 263–276.

Hargreaves, A., & Fullan, M. (1998). *What's worth fighting for out there?* New York: Teachers College Press.

Harris, A. (2002). *School improvement: What's in it for schools?* New York: Routledge-Falmer.

Hasbrouck, J., & Parker, R. (2001). *Quick phonics screener.* College Station, TX: Texas A&M University.

Hord, S. (1992). *Facilitative leadership: The imperative for change.* Austin, TX: Southwest Educational Development Laboratory.

Hord, S. (Ed.). (2004). *Learning together, leading together: Changing schools through professional learning communities.* New York: Teacher's College Press.

Hord, S. M., Rutherford, W. L., Huling-Austin, L., & Hall, G. E. (1987). *Taking charge of change.* Austin, TX: Southwest Educational Development Laboratory.

Hord, S., Stiegelbauer, S., Hall, G., & George, A. (2006). *Measuring implementation in schools: Innovation configurations.* Austin, TX: Southwest Educational Development Laboratory.

Huberman, M. (1983). Recipes for busy kitchens. *Knowledge: Creation, Diffusion, Utilization, 4,* 478–510.

Hughes, J. N. (2003). Commentary: Participatory action research leads to sustainable school and community improvement. *School Psychology Review, 32*(1), 38–43.

Isaacson, W. (2007). *Einstein: His life and universe.* New York: Simon & Schuster.

Johnson, R. S. (2002). *Using data to close the achievement gap: How to measure equity in our schools.* Thousand Oaks, CA: Corwin Press.

John-Steiner, V., Weber, R., & Minnis, M. (1998). The challenge of studying collaboration. *American Educational Research Journal, 35*(4), 773–783.

Joyce, B., Wolf, J., & Calhoun, E. (1993). *The self-renewing school.* Alexandria, VA: Association for Supervision and Curriculum Development.

Kalyanpur, M., & Harry, B. (1997). A posture of reciprocity: A practical approach to collaboration between professionals and parents of culturally diverse backgrounds. *Journal of Child and Family Studies, 6,* 487–509.

Kember, D., Ha, T., Lam, B., Lee, A., Ng, S., Yan, L., & Yum, J. C. K. (1997). The diverse role of the critical friend in supporting educational action research projects. *Educational Action Research, 5*(3), 463–481.

Kemmis, S., & McTaggart, R. (2005). Participatory action research: Communicative action and the public sphere. In N. Denzin & Y. Lincoln (Eds.), *Handbook of qualitative research* (3rd ed., pp. 559–603). Thousand Oaks, CA: Sage Publications.

Kreisberg, S. (1992). *Transforming power: Domination, empowerment and education.* Albany: State University of New York Press.

Lambert, L. (2005). What does leadership capacity really mean? *Journal of Staff Development, 26*(2), 38–40.

Lather, P. (1986). Issues of validity in openly ideological research: Between a rock and a soft place. *Interchange, 17*(4), 63–84.

Lather, P. (1991). *Getting smart: Feminist research and pedagogy with/in the (post) modern.* New York: Routledge.

Levin, H. M. (1986). *Educational reform for disadvantaged students: An emerging crisis.* West Haven, CT: NEA Professional Library.

Lewin, K. (1948). *Resolving social conflicts: Selected papers on group dynamics* (G. W. Lewin, Ed.). New York: Harper & Row.

Lieberman, A., & Miller, L. (1992). *Teachers—Their world and their work: Implications for school improvement.* New York: Teachers College Press.

Little, J. W. (1982). Norms of collegiality and experimentation: Workplace conditions of school success. *American Educational Research Journal, 19*(3), 325–340.

Lovely, S. (2005). Making the leap to shared leadership. *Journal of Staff Development, 26*(2), 16–21.

Lunsford, B. (1995). A league of our own. *Educational Leadership, 52*(7), 59–61.

MacBeath, J. (1998). I didn't know he was ill—The role and value of the critical friend. In L. Stoll & K. Myers (Eds.), *No quick fixes: Perspectives on schools in difficulty* (pp. 118–132). London: Falmer Press.

MacBeath, J. (1999). *Schools must speak for themselves: The case for school self-evaluation.* London: Routledge.

MacBeath, J., & Myers, K. (1999). *Effective school leaders.* London: Pearson.

Marris, P. (1975). *Loss and change.* New York: Anchor Press/Doubleday.

Marzano, R. (2003). *What works in schools: Translating research into action.* Alexandria, VA: Association for Supervision and Curriculum Development.

McGhee, M. (1992). *Relation of leadership temperament to change facilitator effectiveness.* Unpublished doctoral dissertation, University of Texas, Austin.

McLaughlin, C., & Black-Hawkins, K. (2004). A schools–university research partnership: Understandings, models and complexities. *Journal of In-Service Education, 30*(2), 265–283.

McLaughlin, H. J., Watts, C., & Beard, M. (2000). Just because it's happening doesn't mean it's working: Using action research to improve practice in middle schools. *Phi Delta Kappan, 82*(4), 284–290.

Merriam, S. B., & Simpson, E. L. (2000). *A guide to research for educators and trainers of adults* (2nd ed.). Malabar, FL: Krieger.

Miles, M. B. (1992, April). *40 Years of change in schools: Some personal reflections.* Paper presented at the annual meeting of the American Educational Research Association, San Francisco.

Miles, M. B., & Huberman, A. M. (1994). *Qualitative data analysis* (2nd ed.). Thousand Oaks, CA: Sage Publications.

Miles, M. B., Saxi, E. R., & Lieberman, A. (1988). What skills do educational change agents need? An empirical view. *Curriculum Inquiry, 18*(2), 157–193.

Minnis, M., John-Steiner, V., & Weber, R. (1994). *Collaborations: Values, roles and working methods* [Research proposal]. Albuquerque, NM: National Science Foundation, Ethics and Values Program.

Moss, C. M. (1997, March). *Systematic self-reflection: Professional development for the reflective practitioner.* Paper presented at the annual meeting of the American Educational Research Association, Chicago, IL.

Muijs, D., Harris, A., Chapman, C., Stoll, L., & Russ, J. (2004). Improving schools in socioeconomically disadvantaged areas—A review of research evidence. *School Effectiveness and School Improvement, 15*(2), 149–175.

Murphy, C. (1997). Finding time for faculties to study together. *Journal of Staff Development, 18*(3), 29–32.

Murphy, C. E. (1999). Use time for faculty study. *Journal of Staff Development, 20*(2), 20–25.

National Association of Secondary School Principals. (2004). *Breaking ranks II: Strategies for leading high school reform.* Reston, VA: Author.

National College for School Leadership. (n.d.). *Network leadership in action: What does a critical friend do?* Retrieved July 9, 2007, from http://www.ncsl.org.uk/networked/networked-n.cfm

National Governors Association. (2007, February 28). *National summit on America's "silent epidemic" to highlight America's response to the dropout crisis* [News release].

National Research Council. (1996). *National science education standards.* Washington, DC: National Academies Press.

National Research Council. (2004). *Engaging schools: Fostering high school students' motivation to learn.* Washington, DC: National Academies Press.

National School Reform Faculty. (n.d.). *Program description.* Retrieved July 13, 2007, from http://www.nsrfarmony.org/program.html

Newman, S. B., & Roskos, K. (1994). Bridging home and school with a culturally responsive approach. *Childhood Education, 70*, 210–214.

O'Neal, S., Nelson, S. W., Gaines, L., & Valentino, A. (2004). Literacy learning for every child in an urban classroom: Can we raise scores and scholars? In D. Lapp, C. Block, E. Cooper, J. Flood, N. Roser, & J. Tinajero (Eds.), *Teaching all the children: Strategies for developing literacy in an urban setting* (pp. 153–160). New York: Guilford Press.

Organization for Economic Cooperation and Development. (2007). *Education at a glance 2007*. Retrieved June 10, 2008, from http://www.oecd.org/dataoecd/17/31/39245343.xls.

Patterson, J., Purkey, S., & Parker, J. (1986). *Productive school systems for a nonrational world*. Alexandria, VA: Association for Supervision and Curriculum Development.

Patton, M. Q. (2002). *Qualitative research and evaluation methods* (3rd ed.). Thousand Oaks, CA: Sage Publications.

Perchemlides, N., & Coutant, C. (2004). Growing beyond grades. *Educational Leadership, 62*(2), 53–56.

Poetter, T. S. (1997). *Voices of inquiry in teacher education*. Mahwah, NJ: Lawrence Erlbaum.

Quint, J. (2006). Research-based lessons from high school reform: Findings from three models. *Principal's Research Review, 1*(3), 1–8.

Race, R. (2002). Teacher professionalism or deprofessionalisation? The consequences of school-based management on domestic and international contexts. [Thematic review of the books *Teachers and the state: Towards a directed profession; Teachers work in a globalizing economy;* and *School based management.*] *British Educational Research Journal, 28*(3), 459–463.

Raptis, H., & Fleming, T. (2005, January 31). Using action research in British Columbia. Preliminary findings from school improvement projects in seven schools, 2002–2004. *International Electronic Journal for Leadership in Learning, 9*(1). Retrieved June 28, 2006, from http://www.ucalgary.ca/niej22

Reason, P. (2004). Critical design ethnography as action research. *Anthropology and Education Quarterly, 35*(2), 269–276.

Reason, P., & Bradbury, H. (2001). Introduction: Inquiry and participation in search of a world worthy of human aspiration. In P. Reason & H. Bradbury (Eds.), *Handbook of action research: Participative inquiry and practice* (pp. 1–14). London: Sage Publications.

Rhodes, D., Smerdon, B., Burt, W., Evan, A., Martinez, B., & Means, B. (2005). *Getting to results: Student outcomes in new and redesigned high schools*. Washington, DC: American Institutes for Research.

Robbins, P. (1991). *How to plan and implement a peer coaching program*. Alexandria, VA: Association for Supervision and Curriculum Development.

Robelen, E. W. (2005). Gates high schools get mixed review in study. *Education Week, 25*(12), 1.

Rosenholtz, S. (1989). *Teachers' workplace*. New York: Longman.

Rowan, B., & Miller, R. (2007). Organizational strategies for promoting instructional change: Implementation dynamics in schools working with comprehensive school reform providers. *American Educational Research Journal, 44*(2), 252–297.

Roy, P., & Hord, S. (2003). Moving NSDC's staff development standards into practice: Innovation configurations. Oxford, OH: National Staff Development Council.

Rust, F. O., & Freidus, H. (2001). *Guiding school change: The role and work of change agents*. New York: Teachers College Press.

Sagor, R. (1991). What project LEARN reveals about collaborative action research. *Educational Leadership, 48*(6), 6–10.

Sagor, R. (2000). *Guiding school improvement with action research.* Alexandria, VA: Association for Supervision and Curriculum Development.

Sarason, S. B. (1990). *The predictable failure of educational reform: Can we change before it's too late?* San Francisco: Jossey-Bass.

Sarason, S. B. (1996). *Revisiting the culture of the school and the problem of change.* New York: Teachers College Press.

Schaefer, R. J. (1967). *The school as a center of inquiry.* New York: Harper and Row.

Schlechty, P. (2002). *Working on the work: An action plan for teachers, principals, and superintendents.* San Francisco: Jossey-Bass.

Schmoker, M. (2004). Tipping point: From feckless reform to substantive instructional improvement. *Phi Delta Kappan, 85*(6), 424–432.

Schoenfeld, A. H. (1999). Looking toward the 21st century: Challenges of educational theory and practice. *Educational Researcher, 28*(7), 4–14.

Schuck, S., & Russell, T. (2005). Self-study, critical friendship, and the complexities of teacher education. *Studying Teacher Education, 1*(2), 107–121.

Scribner, J. D., & Reyes, P. (1999). Creating learning communities for high-performing Hispanic students: A conceptual framework. In P. Reyes, J. D. Scribner, & A. P. Scribner (Eds.), *Lessons from high-performing Hispanic schools: Creating learning communities* (pp. 188–210). New York: Teachers College Press.

Scribner, J. D., Young, M. D., & Pedroza, A. (1999). Building collaborative relationships with parents. In P. Reyes, J. D. Scribner, & A. P. Scribner (Eds.), *Lessons from high-performing Hispanic schools: Creating learning communities* (pp. 36–60). New York: Teachers College Press.

Senge, P., Cambron-McCabe, N., Lucas, T., Smith, B., Dutton, J., & Kleiner, A. (2000). *Schools that learn: A Fifth Discipline fieldbook for educators, parents, and everyone who cares about education.* New York: Doubleday.

Shear, L., Song, M., House, A., Martinez, B., Means, B., & Smerdon, B. (2005). *Creating cultures for learning: Supportive relationships in new and redesigned high schools.* Washington, DC: American Institutes for Research.

Shirley, D. (1997). *Community organizing for urban school reform.* Austin: University of Texas Press.

Sizer, T. (1986). Rebuilding: First steps by the Coalition of Essential Schools. *Phi Delta Kappan, 68*(1), 38–42.

Smith, D. (2005). *Institutional ethnography: A sociology for people.* Lanham, MD: Rowman & Littlefield.

Smith, L. (2005). On tricky ground: Researching the native in the age of uncertainty. In N. Denzin & Y. Lincoln (Eds.), *Handbook of qualitative research* (3rd ed., pp. 85–107). Thousand Oaks, CA: Sage Publications.

Smyth, J. (1989). Developing and sustaining critical reflection in teacher education. *Journal of Teacher Education, 40*(2), 2–9.

Smyth, J. (2003a). Undamaging 'damaged' teachers: An antidote to the 'self-managing school.' *Delta: Policy and Practice in Education, 55*(1&2), 15–42.

Smyth, J. (2003b). Engaging the education sector: A policy orientation to stop damaging our schools. *Learning Communities: International Journal of Learning in Social Contexts, 1*(1), 22–40.

Smyth, J. (2005a). Policy research and "damaged teachers": Toward an epistemologically respectful paradigm. In F. Bodone (Ed.), *What difference does research make and for whom?* (pp. 141–159). New York: Peter Lang Publishing.

Smyth, J. (2005b). An argument for new understandings and explanations of early school leaving that go beyond the conventional. *London Review of Education, 3*(2), 117–130.

Smyth, J., & Hattam, R. (with Cannon, J., Edwards, J., Wilson, N., & Wurst, S.). (2004). *'Dropping out', drifting off, being excluded: Becoming somebody without school.* New York: Peter Lang Publishing.

Smyth, J., Hattam, R., Cannon, J., Edwards, J., Wilson, N., & Wurst, S. (2000). *Listen to me, I'm leaving: Early school leaving in South Australian secondary schools.* Adelaide: Flinders Institute for the Study of Teaching; Department of Employment, Education and Training; and Senior Secondary Assessment Board of South Australia.

Smyth, J., & McInerney, P. (2007). *Teachers in the middle: Reclaiming the wasteland of the adolescent years of schooling.* New York: Peter Lang Publishing.

Southeast Comprehensive Assistance Center. (2004). *Coaching for results: Peer coaching study teams to increase professional and student learning.* Retrieved June 27, 2007, from http://www.sedl.org/secac/rsn/peer.pdf

Sparks, D. (2001, Fall). Why change is so challenging for schools: An interview with Peter Senge. *Journal of Staff Development, 22*(3), 42–47.

Spillane, J., Halverson, R., & Diamond, J. (2001). Investigating school leadership practice: A distributed perspective. *Educational Researcher, 30*(3), 23–28.

Stenhouse, L. (1975). *An introduction to curriculum research and development.* London: Heinemann.

Stiegelbauer, S. M. (1996). Change has changed: Implications for implementation. In M. Kane (Ed.), *Implementing performance assessment: Promises, problems, and challenges* (pp. 139–159). Mahwah, NJ: Lawrence Erlbaum.

Stiegelbauer, S. M., Gordon, S. P., & McGhee, M. (2005, April). *Developing capacity for school improvement through a school-university partnership.* Paper presented at the annual meeting of the American Educational Research Association, Montreal.

Stoll, L., & Fink, D. (1998). The cruising school: The unidentified ineffective school. In L. Stoll & K. Myers (Eds.), *No quick fixes: Perspectives on schools in difficulty* (pp. 189–206). London: Falmer Press.

Stringer, E. (1999). *Action research* (2nd ed.). Thousand Oaks, CA: Sage Publications.

Susman, G. I., & Evered, R. D. (1978). An assessment of the scientific merits of action research. *Administrative Science Quarterly, 23*(4), 582–603.

Swaffield, S. (2004a). Critical friends: Supporting leadership, improving learning. *Improving Schools, 7*(3), 267–278.

Swaffield, S. (2004b, January). *Exploring critical friendship through leadership for learning.* Paper presented at the International Congress for School Effectiveness and Improvement, Rotterdam.

Swaffield, S. (2005). No sleeping partners: Relationships between head teachers and critical friends. *School Leadership and Management, 25*(1), 43–57.

Task Force on Teacher Leadership, Institute for Educational Leadership. (2001). *Leadership for Student Learning: Redefining the Teacher as Leader.* Washington, DC: Institute for Educational Leadership. Retrieved May 9, 2008, from http://www.iel.org/programs/21st/reports/teachlearn.pdf

Tierney, W. G. (2002). Parents and families in precollege preparation: The lack of connection between research and practice. *Educational Policy, 16,* 588–606.

Tillotson, J. W. (2000). Studying the game: Action research in science education. *Clearing House, 74*(1), 31–34.

Tobia, E. F., & Hord, S. (2002). *Making the leap: Leadership, learning, and successful program implementation.* Austin, TX: Southwest Educational Development Laboratory.

Torrez, N. (2004). Developing parent information frameworks that support college preparation for Latino students. *The High School Journal, 87*(3), 54–62.

Van den Berg, R. (2002). Teachers' meanings regarding educational practice. *Review of Educational Research, 72*(4), 577–625.

Wasley, P., Hampel, R., & Clark, R. (1997). The puzzle of whole-school change. *Phi Delta Kappan, 78,* 690–697.

Watling, R., Hopkins, D., Harris, A., & Beresford, J. (1998). Between the devil and the deep blue sea? Implications for school and LEA development following an accelerated inspection programme. In L. Stoll & K. Myers (Eds.), *No quick fixes: Perspectives on schools in difficulty* (pp. 47–63). London: Falmer.

Wise, A. (1977). Why educational policies often fail: The hyperrationalization hypothesis. *Curriculum Studies, 9*(1), 43–57.

Yankelovich, D. (1991). *Coming to public judgment: Making democracy work in a complex society.* New York: Syracuse University Press.

Zemelman, S., Daniels, H., & Hyde, A. (1998). *Best practice: New standards for teaching and learning.* Portsmouth, NH: Heinemann.

Zimmerman, J. (2006). Why some teachers resist change and what principals can do about it. *NASSP Bulletin, 90*(6), 238–249.

About the Contributors

MICHAEL BOONE is a Professor of Education and Community Leadership at Texas State University–San Marcos. He received the Ed.D. from Washington State University and has served as a teacher, principal, and superintendent of schools. At Texas State University he teaches educational leadership courses at both the master's and the doctoral levels. His research interests include rural education, educational leadership, and the relationship between education and democracy. Dr. Boone is a member of the National Rural Education Association, the University Council on Educational Administration, the National Council of Professors of Educational Administration, and the Texas Association of School Administrators.

BARBARA DAVIS is an Associate Professor of Curriculum and Instruction at Texas State University–San Marcos. She is Director of the Teacher Fellows, a graduate induction program for beginning teachers. She also teaches undergraduate Reading Education courses in the field-based teacher preparation program. Her research interests include action research, novice teacher induction, and literacy education. Dr. Davis has taught elementary through high school and served as a public and private school administrator. She is the author of numerous articles about teaching and learning.

JULIE DIEHL works for Educational Testing Service in San Antonio, Texas, developing certification tests for Texas teachers. She taught elementary school in central Texas for six years. She received a master's degree in educational administration from Texas State University–San Marcos. Julie was research assistant for the National Center for School Improvement and its School Improvement Network during the action research reported on in this book. She is currently in the dissertation stage of her Education Ph.D. in School Improvement at Texas State.

IRIS ESCANDÓN teaches fifth grade at Jackson Keller Elementary in Northeast Independent School District in San Antonio, Texas. During her career as an educator, she has taught two years in a multiage first/second-grade classroom and three years in a second-grade bilingual classroom. She also served as a math and science specialist. Iris has chaired a bilingual committee and served on various school and district leadership teams. While pursuing a master's degree in Education at Texas State University–San Marcos, she participated as a teacher-leader at one of the School Improvement Network campuses.

STEPHEN P. GORDON is a Professor of Education and Community Leadership at Texas State University–San Marcos. He is editor of the book *Standards for Instructional Supervision: Enhancing Teaching and Learning*, author of the book *Professional Development for School Improvement: Empowering Learning Communities*, and co-author of the books *How to Help Beginning Teachers Succeed*, with Susan Maxey, and *SuperVision and Instructional Leadership: A Developmental Approach*, with Carl D. Glickman, and Jovita M. Ross-Gordon. Steve also was lead consultant for the Association of Supervision and Curriculum Development's video series *Improving Instruction through Observation and Feedback*. Steve received his Ed.D. in Supervision from the University of Georgia.

MIGUEL A. GUAJARDO, Assistant Professor of Education and Community Leadership at Texas State University–San Marcos, conducts research and teaches courses on issues of community-building, leadership development, race and ethnicity, community as pedagogy, action research, and university and community partnerships. Miguel also served as a Fellow with the Kellogg International Leadership Program and has been involved in the Foundation's new generation of leadership development, Kellogg Leadership for Community Change (KLCC). He is also co-founder of the Llano Grande Center for Research and Development and serves as the Co-Chairman of its Board of Directors.

MARLA W. McGHEE is Associate Professor and Director of Educational Leadership Programs at Lewis & Clark College in Portland, Oregon. She worked in the public schools of Texas for 21 years, serving as a teacher, an elementary principal, a secondary principal, and a central office curriculum area director. Under her leadership, Live Oak Elementary School was named a U.S. Department of Education Blue Ribbon School in 1992. She was selected to represent Texas as the National Distinguished Principal in 1994. Her research and writing interests include instructional supervision and leadership, the unintended consequences of educational accountability systems, and the contemporary assistant principalship. She holds two degrees from Texas Tech University and a Ph.D. in Educational Administration from the University of Texas at Austin. Marla is the co-author of *The Principal's Guide to a Powerful Library Media Program.*

SARAH W. NELSON is an Assistant Professor of Education and Community Leadership at Texas State University–San Marcos. She teaches courses in school leadership, research, school law, educational policy, and educational environments. Her research interests include the preparation of culturally responsive educators, educational accountability, and educational equity. Before joining the faculty at Texas State, Sarah served as the principal and instructional leader of a large urban elementary school. She continues to work in the field with educators to develop culturally responsive teaching and learning environments and to create community-based leadership practices.

JANE ROSS serves as a Positive Support Specialist in central Texas. Prior to her current position, she served as an assistant principal, instructional specialist, mathematics teacher, and lead mentor at a diverse urban middle school. Jane earned her Ph.D. in Education with a major in School Improvement from Texas State University–San Marcos, where she recently accepted an adjunct faculty position in the Education and Community Leadership Program. Her areas of interest include: culturally responsive education; new teacher development; sustainable parent and community involvement; sustainable educator commitment; curriculum, instruction, assessment, and professional development alignment; and teacher voice in educational policy-making.

CHARLES L. SLATER is Professor of Educational Administration at California State University–Long Beach. He received his Ph.D. at the University of Wisconsin–Madison and has been superintendent of schools in Texas and

Massachusetts. He has written on educational leadership in the Unites States and Mexico in *Leading and Managing,* the *Journal for Educational Research and Policy Studies,* the *Educational Forum,* the *Journal of School Leadership,* and the *International Journal of Leadership in Education.* He was the College of Education's 2005 nominee for the Presidential Award for Excellence in Teaching at Texas State University–San Marcos.

JOHN SMYTH is Research Professor of Education, School of Education, University of Ballarat, Australia. In 2004–2005 he held the Roy F. and Joann Cole Mitte Endowed Chair in School Improvement, Texas State University–San Marcos. He also is an Emeritus Professor of Flinders University of South Australia. He has recently been appointed the Simon Visiting Professor at University of Manchester. He is a former Senior Fulbright Research Scholar, and in 1992 was awarded the Palmer Johnston award for outstanding research from the American Educational Research Association. He is author/editor of 15 books and has published many scholarly articles. His research interests include: policy ethnographies of schooling, issues of social justice, community renewal, and policy sociology of students' lives and teachers' work.

SUZANNE M. STIEGELBAUER is an Associate Professor at the Ontario Institute for Studies in Education at the University of Toronto (OISE/UT). From 2003 to 2007 she was a member of the faculty at Texas State University–San Marcos. Dr. Stiegelbauer has worked in the area of educational change for over 20 years and has been involved in projects with change researchers such as Shirley Hord, Gene Hall, Susan Loucks-Horsley, Stephen Anderson, Michael Fullan, Ken Leithwood, Stephen Gordon, SEDL, and the U.S. Department of Education. As an anthropologist, her focus has been on the social interactions in change and the dynamics of a change process.

Index

Page numbers followed by *f* and *t* refer to figures and tables, respectively.

200